Bulgaria

Front cover: A wheel of a traditional
wooden cart from Nessebur

Right: A Bulgar warrior

TOP 10 ATTRACTIONS

Alexander Nevski Cathedral • The pride of Bulgaria's capital Sofia, with glittering domes and a fascinating crypt *(page 33)*

Sandstone pyramids • These impressive structures stand guard near Melnik *(page 46)*

Veliko Tarnovo • One of the country's most picturesque cities *(page 61)*

Bachkovo Monastery • A haven of fine religious art and architecture *(page 57)*

Nessebur • The jewel of Bulgaria's Black Sea coast, Nessebur has an excellent beach and a medieval Old Town *(page 77)*

Rila Monastery • A holy site set among the mountains and adorned with gorgeous frescoes *(page 49)*

Bansko • The ski resort has much to offer besides the pleasures of the piste *(page 46)*

Plovdiv • This attractive city fuses history with a lively café and cultural scene *(page 52)*

The National History Museum • Bulgaria's treasurehouse *(page 36)*

Iskar Gorge • Follow its long and spectacular course *(page 39)*

CONTENTS

77

49

66

INTRODUCTION

Long ago, Bulgaria was the most powerful country in Europe. That is a title it no longer has, but it can still lay claim to being one of the most fascinating. It is certainly different. A place where east meets west, it is perhaps fitting that this was one of the few places on earth where, for 40 years, East Germans could meet their West German relatives with ease. All this at a time when Bulgaria was the staunchest ally of the Soviet Union, upholding an orthodox socialist regime, yet also the first Soviet ally to develop its massive potential as a tourist destination. Bulgaria invested heavily in tourism during the 1960s. Purpose-built seaside and ski resorts appeared almost overnight, and the often ridiculously cheap prices attracted a large number of visitors from Western Europe, particularly Britain and Germany.

Life in the slow lane: a glimpse of rural Bulgaria

Since Bulgaria peacefully waved goodbye to Communism in 1990, tourist facilities have become even better. From the beach resorts and fishing villages of the Black Sea to the new ski centre of Bansko; from the provincial-in-size yet cosmopolitan-in-attitude capital of Sofia to the historical region around Veliko Tarnovo, Bulgaria still offers tremendous value for money, while preserving its uniqueness.

Bulgarian national emblem at the Shipka Pass

Bulgaria's 8 million people are slowly coming to terms with their place in contemporary Europe. In the 1990s many Bulgarians voted with their feet, emigrating en masse to Spain and Italy in particular. However, now that Bulgaria is an EU member, with a booming economy and a stable political climate, the country is no longer losing its people at such an alarming rate. Indeed, many of those who left a decade ago are returning.

Nevertheless, in foreign eyes it will be some time before the image of Bulgaria as a Balkan backwater is eroded. But the country has never been backwards, rather a dynamic mix of rural and urban, ancient and modern, traditional and innovative. Whereas in other Balkan countries cultural diversity has had the potential to be destructive, in Bulgaria it has always been celebrated.

Simeon Saxe-Coburg

Former king Simeon Saxe-Coburg served as Bulgaria's prime minister from June 2001 to August 2005. He was the first ex-monarch to return to power, either as monarch or elected politician, in Eastern Europe.

Simeon became king at the age of six after his father's death in 1943, but was banished from the country in 1946 after an allegedly rigged referendum abolished the Bulgarian monarchy. He spent most of his life in Madrid, where he was as a successful businessman. He returned from exile to compete in parliamentary elections in June 2001, and his National Movement for Simeon II (NDSV) won 120 seats in parliament, one short of an outright majority. He led a mildly successful coalition, and Bulgaria was made a member of nato during his term in office.

However, Simeon failed to stamp out corruption, or to significantly increase the standard of living in rural areas. As a result, his centre-right government narrowly lost power in the 2005 election, although his party is part of a grand coalition led by Prime Minister Sergei Stanishev.

The Country and its Climate

Bordered by Romania to the north, Serbia and Macedonia to the west, Greece and Turkey to the south and a deceptively short coastline of 378km (235 miles) along the Black Sea to the east, the Republic of Bulgaria covers some 110,993 sq km (42,855 sq miles), an area about the size of Ireland. The capital, Sofia, where a fifth of the population lives, lies in the west of the country, at the apex of the two great mountain ranges that sweep through the country: the Balkans range, which extends almost to the Black Sea, and the Rila/Rhodopes

Albena, a fashionable Bulgarian seaside resort (see page 75)

range, which runs south into Greece and east into Macedonia. The highest mountain in the country is Mt Moussala, at 2,925m (9,596ft) the tallest in the entire Balkan Peninsula.

Bulgaria suffers from climatic extremes, with winters usually bitterly cold, and summers, especially along the Danube plain, often extremely hot. Average temperatures in Sofia in January range from -4–2°C (25–36°F), while in August they usually climb to over 30°C (86°F). Precipitation levels throughout the year are high. Outside the dry Danube plain, you never have to wait long for a downpour in Bulgaria.

Making a gesture

Bulgarians nod their heads when they mean 'no' and shake their heads when they mean 'yes'. Do not be caught out. Ask a kiosk vendor if she has any bus tickets, and a shake of the head actually means 'as many as you like'. It is easy to get confused.

Population and Language

More than 85 percent of the population speaks the official language, Bulgarian. Another 2.5 percent speaks Macedonian, considered in the country to be a Bulgarian dialect and not a separate language. Bulgarian is written in the Cyrillic alphabet – the traveller would do well to learn the characters – created in the 9th century by two Salonika-based Bulgarian monks, Cyril and Methodius *(see pages 16 and 118)*. So proud are Bulgarians of the alphabet that they have even given it a national holiday (May 24, Education Day). Other minority languages include Turkish – spoken by 9 percent of the population – and the related languages of Gagauz, Tatar and Albanian. Small pockets of Romanian speakers (Vlachs) also exist along the eastern Danube.

The population has declined by as much as a million since 1989, as young Bulgarians migrate to Western Europe in search of their fortunes. The population appears to have steadied, however, a reflection of improving living standards.

The name Bulgaria – land of the Bulgars – is something of a misnomer. Today's Bulgarians are descendants of a number of peoples: the Slavs, Greeks and Macedonians, as well as the Bulgars. Much as the Angles gave their name to England without ever being the most populous group in the country, so the Bulgars were just one of many peoples who formed the Bulgarian state. They were the most astute politically, however, playing one tribe off against another, and they quickly became the ruling class after arriving in the Balkans from an area now known as Old Bulgaria, situated between the Black and Caspian seas.

Religion and Culture

The majority of the population – around 90 percent – is Bulgarian Orthodox. There is a significant Catholic minority, while western Protestantism, in the form of the Baptist and Methodist churches, has become increasingly popular since 1990, and is the country's fastest growing faith. Most of Bulgaria's Turks remain Muslims, although over 250,000 left Bulgaria in the summer of 1989 – mainly for Turkey – during the 'Great Exodus'.

It is perhaps the Bulgarian Orthodox Church that has most strongly influenced Bulgarian culture. But what is specifically Bulgarian and what is merely Balkan? So much culture is shared between all the countries of the region (language, music, folklore, even food) that while the Bulgarians are clearly a different people to the Serbs, for example, it is difficult to gauge what makes them so. Yet there are specific cultural achievements of which Bulgaria is rightfully proud. The Thracians, who emerged in the 2nd millennium BC, were unsurpassed in the exploitation of metals – the best examples are to be found in the Pangyurishte treasure or the frescoes of the Boyana church, work that anticipated the Renaissance. This ancient expertise points to a deeply rooted cultural heritage that has withstood an often violent and turbulent history.

Ceiling fresco from Church of the Virgin Birth, Rila Monastery

Driving in the Trigrad Gorge

Landscape and Wildlife

Bulgaria is blessed with natural wonders. The beaches of the Black Sea are among the finest in Europe. The interior is marked by the great mountain ranges, with plains in between. At the right time of year – the end of April – visitors can enjoy skiing one day and sunbathing the next.

Yet while skiing is popular, mountain hiking remains the preferred pastime and Bulgarians see walking up the nearest mountain as something of a rite of passage. Even during the winter it is not uncommon to see courting couples wandering up or down a piste. The best hiking is offered by the Pirin Mountains, the most spectacular of the Bulgarian ranges, while the Rhodopes offer less demanding hikes. Lovers of lakes head for the Rila range.

Bulgaria's mountains and lowlands are also rich in wildlife, and offer excellent opportunities for birdwatchers. The marshlands around Bourgas (known as the Strandzha) and the Madzharovo nature reserve in the Rhodopes are the best birdwatching areas in the country. Bears are still sometimes seen in parts of the Rila and Rhodope mountains. They are dangerous and you should never try to approach them.

Bulgaria has three national parks: Pirin, Central Balkan and Rila, as well as nine nature reserves, of which two, Pirin and Sreburna, are included on UNESCO's World Heritage list.

A BRIEF HISTORY

History in the Balkans is often less the study of past events and more an examination of national pride, with a good deal of myth and legend thrown in for good measure. Though Bulgaria's history is not exceptional, the simple fact that the Cyrillic alphabet was invented by two Bulgarian monks has ensured that the modern Bulgarian story has been well documented for far longer than that of most other nations in the region.

Thracians, Rome and Byzantium

While there are traces of ancient settlements in Stara Zagora, the history of Bulgaria really begins with the emergence of the Thracians on the Danubian plain around 1200BC. The Thracians were an amalgamation of earlier tribes, who may have migrated to the region from Mesopotamia. Archaeological evidence suggests that there was certainly communication between the Near East and the Balkans across the Black Sea by the end of the 2nd millennium BC.

The first documented history of the region comes from the Greeks, who began to visit Thrace in the 7th and 6th centuries BC, gradually extending their influence from the coast inland. Though Persian invasion briefly disrupted this Hellenisation in the 6th century BC, Philip of Macedonia conquered Thrace in 346BC and began colonising the

Valley of Kings

In 2004 a number of archaeological discoveries were made south of the Stara Planina Mountains in an area dubbed the 'Valley of the Thracian Kings'. The findings include a 2,400-year-old Thracian shrine near Shipka, believed to be the burial chamber of King Seuthes III, rival to Alexander the Great.

Sofia's 4th-century Sv Georgi Rotunda sits amid Roman ruins

area, building settlements, including one that carried his name, Philopopolis, the present-day Plovdiv. Under Philip's son, Alexander the Great, the Thracian interior was fully opened up to Greek settlers and merchants, who over the next 200 years fused with the Thracians to form a distinct ethnic group.

Rome conquered Thrace in AD46 and wasted no time in colonising the area. The region prospered. New towns were settled, including Serdica (Sofia), Augusta Traiana (Stara Zagora) and Durostorum (Silistra). But the Roman Empire became overstretched and in AD260 Dacia (present-day Romania, to the north) was abandoned to Barbarians. Thrace, too, came under constant Barbarian attack. The Roman Empire was split between Rome and Constantinople (Byzantium) in 395, but it was not until the reign of Emperor Justinian I (the Great, 527–65) that imperial authority was once again imposed over all of present-day Bulgaria.

The Slavs

Though Justinian encouraged culture and education, fortified the cities of the border lands and quickly settled Serdica and Philipopolis with great numbers of people, the continued power vacuum in Dacia to the north meant that Thrace remained susceptible to invasion. Barbaric, ill-organised tribes such as the Pechenegs and Avars did not get far, but in the 5th century the Slavs, a much larger tribe, swept into the Balkans.

Their origins are unclear, though they migrated into the Balkans from a region thought to be in Poland and Ukraine, and are the forefathers of present-day Croats, Czechs, Serbs, Slovaks, Slovenes, Poles and Russians, as well as Bulgarians. So immoveable were these Slavs that they were not opposed by the Byzantine rulers, who allowed them to settle.

The First Bulgarian Kingdom

No sooner had the Slavs gained hegemony over Thrace than a new wave of immigrants arrived, this time the Bulgars. Politically astute and brilliant horsemen, the Bulgars were described more than once in Byzantine dispatches as 'barbaric and vulgar'. Originating in a region east of the Black Sea, perhaps as far as the Caspian Sea, the Bulgars followed the Black Sea shore, entering Thrace by the Danube Delta. As many as 250,000 came and, led by Khan Asparuh, they established in 681 the Parvo Bulgarsko Tsarstvo (the First Bulgarian Kingdom). Its capital was Pliska.

A Bulgar warrior

The next 200 years are the most fiercely debated in Bulgaria's history. While many Bulgarian historians insist that the tolerance of the Slavs and the enlightened rule of the Bulgars meant that the two nations fused effortlessly – with the Slavs eventually accepting Bulgar dominance – most Western historians see things differently. They claim that only political expediency – the Bulgars needed Slav support – held the uneasy alliance together.

Simeon the Great

Of all Bulgarian leaders, one remains more revered than any other: Simeon the Great (r. 893–927). During his reign, Bulgaria conquered huge swathes of Europe and became the largest empire on the continent, stretching from Greece to Ukraine, from the Black Sea to the Adriatic. Simeon, who had been schooled in Constantinople and knew the value of a good education, used the newly created Cyrillic alphabet as a means of uniting Slavs. More than a warrior, Simeon was a man who realised the importance of culture in uniting a nation, and his patronage of the arts gave birth to the first real age of Bulgarian literature, painting and sculpture.

Yet Simeon greatly overstretched his resources and on his death left no heir capable of replacing him. The Bulgarian empire collapsed, the country once again falling under the spell of Constantinople.

The Cyrillic Alphabet

Although the alphabet only took one man's name, Cyrillic is the work of two monks: Konstantin-Cyril and his brother Methodius. In 855 the two brothers retired to a monastery in Salonika (in modern Greece) to formulate a satisfactory way of rendering the scriptures into the Slavic language. Seven years later they emerged with a rune-based script known as the Glagolitic alphabet, which they later adapted to create a prototype of today's Cyrillic alphabets. This in turn was finessed by the various Slavic peoples to fit local nuances. Cyrillic is used today in Bulgaria, Serbia, Macedonia, Russia, Belarus, Ukraine, Mongolia, Turkmenistan, Tajikistan and Kyrgystan (see page 118).

The Second Kingdom

Byzantium, however, was by this stage an empire in disarray, and it was not long before the Bulgarians regrouped and reclaimed their country; albeit somewhat reduced in size from its days under Simeon. Two brothers, Peter and Assen, led a Bulgar uprising at Mizia, and declared a new Bulgarian Kingdom, with its capital at Veliko Tarnovo.

Cyril and Methodius, fathers of the Cyrillic script

Assen's son, Tsar Kaloyan, further extended Bulgaria, recapturing Varna in 1204, the year the knights of the Fourth Crusade sacked Constantinople and declared their Holy Eastern Empire. Kaloyan was unimpressed and shortly afterwards defeated the Crusaders and set about creating an empire of his own. He was murdered in a palace coup and replaced by Tsar Boril, briefly, before the far more satisfactory Tsar Assen II took power in 1218. Expansion recommenced and Bulgaria was again – briefly – the size it was under Simeon.

Ottoman Domination and the National Revival

The defeat of the Serbs by the Ottoman Turks at Kosovo Polje (Blackbird Field, in Kosovo) in 1389 sealed the fate of the Balkan Peninsula. In 1393, Veliko Tarnovo was captured by the Turks, and three years later all of Bulgaria became part of the Ottoman Empire. This period of Turkish rule, which lasted nearly 500 years, came to be called the Ottoman Yoke.

The list of atrocities committed by the Turks during the Yoke is a long one. At least half the Bulgarian population was killed or left to starve in the first 50 years following the

Bulgarian freedom fighter
statue at Dryanovo Monastery

conquest, while many of those who survived were forced to convert to Islam – though a good number resisted. Arabic replaced Bulgarian as the official language used at court, and Greek became the language of the church.

The occasional uprisings against the Turks, including those at Veliko Tarnovo in 1598 and 1686, never succeeded in bringing about anything resembling change. It was the dominance of Greek priests, appointed by the Turks to oversee the Bulgarian church, which forced a number of Bulgarian intellectuals to take measures to ensure that the Bulgarian language and a Bulgarian-centred history survived. Many intellectuals, such as Bogdan Bakshev, Archbishop of Sofia, were forced to publish their works outside of Bulgaria. Bakshev's *History of Bulgaria* caused a furore when published in the 17th century, as did Pasii of Hilender's *History of the Slav-Bulgarians* (1762). Both works helped rekindle Bulgarian nationalism in the 19th century – a period known as the National Revival. Economics also played a part in the Revival, as an increasing number of wealthy Bulgarians were able to travel to trade in areas not dominated by Turkey, and in doing so returned with new liberal ideas that were anathema to Bulgaria's rulers.

The Struggle for Independence

In 1859, with Russian help, Romania rid itself of the Turks. Ten years later the Bulgarian Revolutionary Committee (BRCK) was created in Bucharest, uniting disparate nationalists for the first time under one group behind one leader, Vasil Levski. The capture and execution of Levski in 1873 provided the movement with a martyr, and in April 1876 it was ready to launch an uprising against the Turks.

During the April Rising, more than 30,000 rebels died, evoking great sympathy from Russia and the Western powers, which until then had urged Turkey to grant Bulgaria autonomy, not independence. Russia declared war on Turkey in 1877 and, after a year of heavy fighting, the Ottoman Empire was forced to sign the humiliating San Stefano Peace Treaty. On 3 March 1878, Bulgaria declared independence.

The Third Bulgarian Kingdom

The other great powers – Britain, France and Austria-Hungary – were not happy with the treaty, and the Congress of Berlin in July of 1878 reversed much of the San Stefano Treaty. Macedonia was returned to Turkey in its entirety, while the rest of the country was divided, creating two provinces that had to pay annual tributes to the Sultan of Turkey, while remaining nominally independent.

Searching Europe for a monarch, the Bulgarian assembly chose Alexander Battenberg to serve as prince, who repaid them by creating an autocratic state in which he wielded considerable power. He is remembered favourably, however, for managing to reunite the divided country (in 1885) very much against the will of Britain and France. He was replaced as prince on his death in 1887 by Ferdinand Saxe-Coburg, who changed his title from prince to tsar in 1908. In the same year Bulgaria again proclaimed full independence from Turkey, and with the Ottoman Empire in chaos, nobody objected.

Sofia's Sv Nedelya Church was bombed by terrorists in 1925

The Balkan Wars and the Difficult 1920s

Bulgaria united with Serbia and Greece in an alliance designed to rid the Balkans of the Turks forever. The First Balkan War of 1912 saw them achieve that goal, almost capturing Istanbul in the process. Then the victors fought between themselves over the spoils in 1913, Bulgaria suffering defeat at the hands of erstwhile allies Serbia and Greece. As a result Macedonia was lost to Serbia, and the Dobruja was lost to Romania.

World War I saw the vast majority of the population side with Russia and its allies, while the government – a sworn enemy of Serbia, Russia's ally – backed the Axis powers. The result was carnage, and defeat in September 1918, after which deserting soldiers attempted a coup, which failed, though it did force Ferdinand to abdicate in favour of his son, Boris III.

Macedonian nationalists of the Internal Macedonian Revolutionary Organisation (IMRO) were a thorn in Bulgaria's side throughout the early 1920s. Opposed to the newly created Yugoslavia, the IMRO was hostile to the policies of Prime Minister Alexander Stamboliski, who sought peaceful coexistence with Yugoslavia. In alliance with military officers, who also opposed the prime minister, the IMRO staged a coup in 1923, killing Stamboliski and creating a shaky coalition that managed to hang on to power, with Boris III still nominally the head of state, until 1935. In November of that year, Boris decided he had had enough of politicians and dismissed the lot, creating an absolute monarchy.

World War II

Bulgaria sided with Germany for a second time in 1941, though the country remained to all intents and purposes neutral, refusing to send troops to the Russian front despite German protestations to do so. There was a German military presence in the country throughout the war, however, and as the tide turned and the Red Army swept through the Balkans in 1944, Bulgaria was quick to see which way the wind was blowing, changing sides on 9 September 1944, a date that is still celebrated as Liberation Day.

Communism

With the Red Army firmly in control of the country, it was impossible for Bulgaria to avoid a post-war Communist takeover. Bulgarian Communists who had fled to Moscow in the 1920s and who had survived Stalin's purges now returned, led by Georgi Dimitrov, who had been leader of the Comintern in the 1930s. Elected in a mockery of an election as prime minister in 1946, Dimitrov immediately had a Communist Party-dominated parliament rubber stamp a new constitution (based on that of the Soviet Union), which abolished the monarchy and created the People's Republic of Bulgaria.

Thompson village

A tiny village in the Iskar Gorge is named after Major Frank Thompson, sent to Bulgaria to evaluate the fighting potential of the local partisans during World War II. Thompson, a committed Marxist, quickly went native and was killed fighting alongside the partisans in 1944. After the war, he was revered by the Bulgarian Communist regime as an anti-fascist hero, and though many cities, towns and villages in Bulgaria that carried Communist-era names have now had their former names restored, the village of Thompson remains Thompson.

Dimitrov died in 1949 and was replaced by Valko Chervenkov, who continued Dimitrov's work by eradicating all actual or potential opponents, most of whom perished in the death camps of Belene, on the Danube. Chervenkov fell out of favour with Moscow after Stalin's death in 1953 and was soon replaced by Todor Zhivkov, who remained Bulgaria's absolute ruler until 1989. Zhivkov's rule is marked by little except utter subservience to the Soviet Union and economic stagnation.

Return to Democracy

Eastern Europe's year of revolutions and political change that was 1989 looked at first to have passed Bulgaria by and, as late as November, Zhivkov's grip on power appeared as tight as ever. He was undone, however, by reformers inside the Communist Party, who on 10 November forced him to resign, arresting him on charges of fraud. The reformers, who had overseen small but significant changes in Bulgaria's economy from the mid-1980s onwards, elected Peter Mladenov as the new head of the Central Committee, promising multi-party elections for June 1990. Since then Bulgaria has struggled with the transition from planned to market economy, but has remained politically stable. Simeon Saxe-Coburg, who was king briefly in the 1940s, oversaw Bulgaria's entry to NATO, but failed to deal with rampant corruption. He was voted out in 2005 to make way for the left-leaning Sergei Stanishev, who heads a grand coalition which successfully negotiated Bulgaria's entry to the EU in January 2007.

The Central Committee Building – now government offices

Historical Landmarks

c. 1200 Emergence of Thrace as an organised state.

356 Philip of Macedonia conquers Thrace.

681 First Bulgarian Kingdom.

855–62 Cyril and Methodius create the Cyrillic alphabet.

865 Christianity adopted as state religion.

927 The Bulgarian Empire reaches its zenith under Simeon the Great.

1018 Emperor Basil II conquers Bulgaria and makes it part of Byzantium.

1185 Second Bulgarian Kingdom created.

1396 Bulgaria becomes part of the Ottoman Empire.

1491 Rila Monastery decorated.

1732 Rozhen Monastery rebuilt.

1876 April Uprising by nationalists put down by Turkey.

1877 Russo-Turkish Wars of Liberation.

1878 Bulgaria declares independence from Turkey.

1879 Sofia becomes capital of Bulgaria.

1912–13 Balkan Wars: Bulgaria, Serbia and Greece unite to defeat the Turkish Empire before fighting each other over the spoils.

1914 Bulgaria sides with the Axis powers in World War I.

1923 Military coup overthrows left-leaning government.

1935 Tsar Boris III declares an absolute monarchy.

1941 Bulgaria enters World War II on the side of Germany.

1944 Soviet Union conquers Bulgaria.

1946 Communists take power after rigged elections.

1953 Todor Zhivkov becomes leader of Bulgaria.

1955 Bulgaria is a founding member of the Warsaw Pact and COMECON.

1978 Bulgarian agents kill émigré dissident Georgi Markov on Waterloo Bridge in London by stabbing him with a poisoned umbrella.

1989 More than 250,000 Turks flee to Turkey; Zhivkov dismissed as leader.

1990 Reformed Communists win general elections.

2004 Bulgaria joins NATO.

2005 Sergei Stanishev elected prime minister.

2007 Bulgaria joins the EU on 1 January.

WHERE TO GO

The best of Bulgaria comprises the capital, Sofia, and the Rila and Pirin mountains to the south; the historically significant Balkan range that sweeps through the centre of the country; and the Black Sea coast. Using the country's three largest cities of Sofia, Plovdiv and Varna, as well as the smaller but regionally important Veliko Tarnovo, as bases – all with excellent hotel, restaurants and services – most of the country can be explored quite easily. And wherever you go, you are seldom far from a sight of historical or natural significance.

SOFIA

Overlooked from the south by the 2,290-m (7,515-ft) high Cerni Vrah, **Sofia** (София; Sofija) nestles snugly at an altitude of just under 600m (1,970ft). Home to one and a half million people, almost a fifth of the country's total population, it has a history going back to the Roman settlement of Serdica, but almost all of its important buildings and monuments, like the modern state they help define, are less than 150 years old. Visitors arriving either by road from the airport or by train will be disappointed

Street names

Some useful terms to know when navigating the streets of Bulgaria's cities, towns and villages are: *bulevard (bul)* – boulevard or avenue; *ploshtad (pl)* – square; and *ulitsa (ul)* – street. You'll find that churches are usually named after a saint: *sveti/sveta (sv)*.

at their first impressions of the Bulgarian capital. Sofia requires a little perseverance from the visitor, for once through

The Petrich Church perches on the hillside at Assenovgrad

the encirclement of monolithic, dilapidated Soviet-era apartment blocks, the city centre is a gem.

Most sights are contained within the area bordered by boulevards Evlogi Georgiev, Hristo Botev, Slivnitsa and Vasil Levski. This area can be divided into three different (though not distinct) districts: **Imperial Sofia**, centred on the Nevski Cathedral, St Sofia and the Yellow Brick Road, **Byzantine and Ottoman Sofia**, around Sveta Nedelya, the Sheraton Hotel and Banya Bashi Mosque, and **Modern Sofia**, the city's commercial hub along boulevards Vitosha and Graf Ignatiev.

Modern Sofia

Modern central Sofia, which stretches from the inner ring road to ploshtad Sveta Nedelya (St Nedelya Square), is by no means an architectural wonder. There are few more modern buildings in the city than the magnificently ugly **National**

Bustling Vitosha Boulevard

Palace of Culture, known by locals and marked on most maps as the **NDK**. Built in 1981 as a multi-purpose cultural venue, it stands guard at the southern entrance to the city centre – it cannot be missed – without a single redeeming feature.

The area in front of the NDK is known as **pl Bulgaria**, or **Yuzhen Park**. It was recently given a facelift, and is now the site of some decent summer terraces, but there is no disguising the fact that it is a concrete wasteland. Though the fountains are attractive (when they are working), the square is dominated by the enormous, eye-catching (for all the wrong reasons) **1,300 Years of Bulgaria Monument**. This folly was conceived in the early 1980s when the Bulgarian Communist Party was reinventing itself as a more nationalist movement. Links with Bulgaria's glorious past, however tenuous, were encouraged. The monument commemorates the anniversary of the founding of the 'first unitary Bulgarian state' in 681, after Khan Asparuh defeated a Byzantine army at the Danube Delta.

Straight ahead you will find **Vitosha Boulevard**, Sofia's main shopping street. Vitosha has long been a centre of commerce, and the street is pleasant enough on the eye, with most of the post-World War II buildings being no taller than four or five storeys. Shops, cafés, street traders and surprisingly wide pavements make a stroll along Vitosha a pleasant experience.

At the northern end of Vitosha is the city's only pedestrian street, **Pirotska**. Lined with cafés and shops, it is worth

Stray dogs

Sofia has a large stray dog population. Though the dogs rarely bite, they do sometimes attack passers by, and young children are particularly at risk. It is to be hoped that the authorities will soon rid the country of this problem. They have failed to do so until now because of objections by the local population of dog lovers. Should you be bitten, go to the nearest hospital for a rabies injection immediately.

exploring for bargains. Running parallel to Pirotska is Ekzarh Yosif, where you will find Sofia's **synagogue**, the largest in the Balkans. Built between 1903–09 the synagogue (open Sun–Fri 9.30am–4pm, except Passover) can accommodate 1,200 worshippers. Today, however, most services are held in the smaller rooms at the front, as Sofia's Jewish population has dwindled to below 5,000 from around 50,000 before World War II.

At the far end of Pirotska is the city's largest market, **Zhenski Pazar**, or women's market (open daily sunrise–sunset). Selling mainly produce, the market also has a number of clothes, craft and bric-a-brac stalls selling good souvenirs, though you may have to hunt through a large amount of tat to find something worthwhile. The real charm of the market is just watching the locals shop.

Sofia's synagogue

A better place to look for bargains is **Graf Ignatiev Boulevard**, which runs at a 45-degree angle from Vitosha to the river. Close to the southern end of Graf Ignatiev is the decrepit-looking **Sv Sedmotchislenitsi Church**, which is dedicated to Saints Cyril and Methodius, the Bulgarian brothers who created the Cyrillic alphabet *(see pages 16 and 118)*. Although less than impressive from the outside, the church's interior is exceptional, with well-preserved frescoes.

Byzantine and Ottoman Sofia

At its northern end, Vitosha Boulevard leads into **pl Sv Nedelya**, the traditional heart of the city, dominated today by the Sheraton Sofia Hotel Balkan, though there is much more to its charms than that splendid building alone.

Sv Sedmotchislenitsi Church

The centrepiece of the square is the church that shares its name, **Sv Nedelya**, which stands on what was the very centre of ancient Serdica. This 19th-century building is the latest in a long line of churches on the site since the Middle Ages. The outside is not impressive, but the inquisitive visitor is rewarded on entering by some of the finest icons and most colourful murals in the country. On leaving, note the plaque that commemorates (in Bulgarian) the fact that assassins attempted to kill Tsar Boris III here by planting a bomb in the church during a service in 1925 *(see picture on page 20)*.

The **Sheraton Hotel Balkan**, behind and to the right of Sv Nedelya, is part of a much larger building; the rear is occupied by the **Presidency** (entry only by appointment), the offices of Bulgaria's president. The two guards who ceremoniously stand erect at the modern glass entrance are an anachronism in their *ancien regime* costumes, but a picture-postcard sight nonetheless.

Directly next to the hotel is **TZUM**, once the state-run department store selling little of any interest to anyone, today a modern, multi-level shopping centre playing host to a wealth of big brand name stores. Across the road is the ghastly **Statue of Sofia**, put up in haste on a whim of the mayor in 2001.

To the right of TZUM in the centre of a small park is Sofia's only surviving, working mosque, the **Banya Bashi**. On the other side of the same square, behind graffiti-strewn hoardings, are the once-majestic **Municipal Baths**, which will remain closed to the public for the foreseeable future while meticulous renovation is carried out on a building that has lain derelict for some time.

Directly opposite the baths is the **Halite** (open daily 6am–8pm), the city's century-old central food market. Recently renovated, the Halite has all kinds of local food inside, from meat and fish to cheese and sweets. The lower level has been expertly adapted to incorporate Serdica ruins, which now act as a backdrop for lunching locals making use of a number of fast-food outlets.

Past the entrance to the Presidency is a large courtyard which hides the city's oldest building, the **Sv Georgi Rotunda**

The Halite food market

(open Mon–Sun 8am–5pm; donations expected). Built for an unknown purpose in the 4th century, it became a church in the 6th century and is today surrounded by part of Sofia's visible **Roman ruins**. Much of what you see on the outside of the rotunda, however, is relatively new, and major restoration work – completed in 1998 – was not always carried out with as much care as it could have been. The Roman ruins look similarly out of context

Soviet-style police car

surrounded by red brick. The real glory of the rotunda lies in its interior: three layers of original frescoes can still be seen, the oldest dating back to the 10th century.

Opposite the Presidency is Sofia's **Archaeological Museum** (open Tues–Sun 10am–6pm; admission fee), which is housed in a recently restored mosque. While there are undoubted treasures within (including two enormous Roman sarcophagi), more work needs to be done and the museum is currently rather disorganised.

The monumental building on the other side of the road is the former Communist Party **Central Committee Building**, from where Bulgaria was run for the best part of 50 years. The building was topped by an enormous red star during the Communist era, and a rather limp flag today tries hard to fill the breach.

Moving further along, the **Largo**, or **Yellow Brick Road** (because of the yellow cobbles), occupied mainly by foreign embassies and government offices, leads to the **Tsar's Former Palace**, today the Ethnographical and National Art Museums *(see below)*, on the right, opposite the recently renovated **Alexander Battenberg Square**. Until 1999, the centrepiece of the square was the stark mausoleum of Georgi Dimitrov, the first Communist leader of Bulgaria who died in 1949. Dimitrov's remains were removed in 1990, and the building itself nine years later. The southern end of the square has a host of good cafés and restaurants, almost all of which have terraces during the summer, while the outdoor café in front of Bulgaria's **National Theatre** on the eastern side is one of the best, trendiest and most expensive places to drink coffee in the city.

Walking back to the Tsar's Former Palace at the northern end of the square, the two museums now housed inside are worth visiting, depending on what's on. The **National Art Gallery** (open Tues–Sun 10am–6pm; admission fee) has no permanent exhibition, and changing exhibitions highlight the works of the country's leading artists, for which guided tours are available in English, with notice, during the week. Far better is the **Ethnographical Musuem** (open Tues–Sun 10am–6pm; admission fee), which includes a good selection of Bulgarian traditional clothes and costumes, arts, crafts and musical instruments. Children in particular will love it. The small gift shop sells good-value souvenirs.

Sv Nikolai Church

Turning left out of the palace, the next building on the left is **Sv Nikolai (Russian) Church**. Built quickly over the winter of 1912–13 on the whim of a Russian diplomat, it is the loveliest church in the city, as its relatively small size prevents it from being overwhelmed by the ostentation that smothers many other churches. The onion domes that give

Alexander Nevski Cathedral

away its heritage were recently repainted in gold leaf donated by Mother Russia. The church's most interesting facet is the **crypt** (open daily 7.30am–6pm), which houses the body of Bishop Serafin, a popular local religious leader who died in 1950, and who was too revered by the local population to be buried in the anonymous grave the recently installed Communist regime wanted.

Imperial Sofia

The Third Kingdom of Bulgaria did not last long. Yet from independence from Turkey in 1878 to the exile of King Simeon II in 1946, regal Bulgaria embarked on a campaign of building and modernising its capital that was at once breathtaking in its speed and impressive in its lasting grandeur.

Of all Sofia's wonders the **Alexander Nevski Cathedral** (open daily 6am–9pm), which stands in a square of the same name, remains the most enduring. Its immaculate golden domes, recently restored to their original splendour with gold leaf donated by the Russian Orthodox Church, still dominate the city's skyline and glitter in any amount of sunlight; even a dull day can be brightened by their sparkle. Built between

1882 and 1912 in the elaborate neo-Byzantine style of the time, the cathedral is named after St Alexander Nevski, the Russian tsar who led his country to victory over Sweden in 1240. He was the patron saint of Tsar Alexander II, the Russian monarch at the time of the cathedral's construction.

The **Alexander Nevski Crypt** (open Tues–Sun, 10.30am–6pm; admission fee), entered down the stairs on the right-hand side of the church's main doors, is the best museum in Sofia and possibly the top attraction in the country. The collection of Old Bulgarian art on show is outstanding, and there are few museums offering a better selection of iconography anywhere in the world. Highlights include the altar doors from the Pogonovo Monastery, dating from 1620, as well as the doors from the Orlitso Nunnery at the Rila Monastery, paintings executed in 1719. All exhibits have captions in Bulgarian and English, and there is an excellent shop selling fine replicas and other Bulgarian souvenirs.

In front of the cathedral is Sofia's oldest church, the **Sv Sofia** (open daily 8am–6pm), which gave the capital its name. Built in the 5th century on the highest point in the city, the

Vasil Levski

On his execution in 1873, the Bulgarian revolutionary Vasil Levski became a martyr for the Bulgarian independence movement; today he is remembered as the country's greatest revolutionary and his name adorns streets, stadiums, monuments and sports teams. Born in 1837, Levski became a professional revolutionary in his early 20s, and quickly became the symbolic leader of the Bulgarian nationalists, travelling in secret around the country to raise funds and find recruits. He was betrayed by Dimitar Obshti, who, when arrested in December 1872, told the Turks all he knew about the Bulgarian revolutionary movement. Levski was arrested and hanged in Sofia the following February; the spot is marked by the Levski Monument.

church has been destroyed and rebuilt a number of times. The Turks used it as a mosque from the 16th century onwards. The present building dates from the late 19th century, built to replace the previous structure (which had a minaret), which was destroyed in Sofia's last great earthquake in 1858.

The city's oldest church and namesake, Sv Sofia

The area between Sv Sofia and the cathedral is dominated by a small but infinitely interesting **flea market**, the perfect place to buy those Todor Zhivkov portraits, Orders of Lenin medals and Hermann Goering fountain pens.

Opposite the cathedral is the **Bulgarian Parliament** building, while behind is the **National Library**, with **Sofia University** next to that on the other side of pl 19 Fevruary. The strange statue at the northern end is in fact the much heralded **Vasil Levski Monument**. This peculiar erection marks the spot where Levski was hanged in 1873 by the Turks for allegedly planning an anti-Ottoman revolt.

Sofia's Outskirts

Sofia offers a number of delights away from the bustle of the city centre, in the hills that lead up towards Vitosha National Park. The most important, and one of the essential stops on any trip to Bulgaria, is **Boyana Church** in the suburb of Boyana, a 20-minute taxi ride (no more than 12 leva) from the city centre (open Tues–Sun 9.30am–5.30pm; admission fee, tours in English and other languages available at extra cost).

Thracian gold at Boyana

Listed by UNESCO as a World Heritage Cultural Site, Boyana was built over two centuries from around 1050 to 1259, when the frescoes for which it is famed were executed. More than 250 people are depicted on the walls in a style that anticipates the Renaissance. The identity of the painter is unknown.

Armed with a good map you can make your way on foot in about 20 minutes from Boyana to the splendid **National History Museum** (open daily 9.30am–5.30pm; admission fee). Walk back from Boyana to the Daskal Sv Popandreev and follow bul Pushkin to where it meets ul Radev. The huge building on the right-hand side, well hidden behind a tall fence and enormous garden complex, is the Boyana residence, the former home of the Communist Party boss **Todor Zhivkov**. The entrance to the museum, housed in a smaller building, is easily found by taking ul Gabrovnitsa, the first turning on the right as you pass the residence. If you don't fancy the downhill walk, you won't have to wait long for a taxi at Boyana, as visitors come and go all the time. You can also take the infrequent bus No. 63 from church to museum.

The National History Museum was relocated to its current Boyana setting in 2000. The move caused a scandal at the time, but the judgment of the city's authorities has proved to be sound. The museum's former home in the Palace of Justice in the centre of town was cramped and dark, whereas the present location allows the stunning collection of well over 22,000 exhibits to breathe. The museum is well laid out, and many of the best exhibits have English captions, though maps showing the Bulgarian Empire's rise and fall are captioned in Bulgarian only. Familiarity with the Cyrillic alphabet *(see page 118)* would help here. Highlights include jewellery dating from 500BC, the Pangyurishte treasure – 6kg (13lb) of gold commissioned by Thracian King Seuthes III – and much early Christian iconography. Children will enjoy the small play area in the rear of the museum, as well as the MIG fighter jets that are on display at the front.

Getting back to the centre of Sofia from the museum is easy: take trolley bus No. 2 from its terminus at the car dealership directly opposite the museum to pl Makedonia.

Todor Zhivkov

Bulgaria's former Stalinist leader Todor Zhivkov cut a sorry figure in the 1990s, one far removed from the hated dictator who had terrorised a country for nearly 40 years. Zhivkov assumed leadership of the Bulgarian Communist Party in 1954, having outmanoeuvred his rivals following the death of Georgi Dimitrov in 1949. Zhivkov's leadership was characterised by slavish loyalty to the Soviet Union, often at the expense of Bulgaria's own interests.

Of all Zhivkov's disastrous policies, which contributed to the utter bankruptcy of the economy, it was his treatment of Bulgaria's Turkish population that secured him a place in the pantheon of the most despised Communist leaders. During the 1970s and 1980s Turks were persecuted mercilessly by Zhivkov's regime until, in the summer of 1989, hundreds of thousands voted with their feet and headed for Turkey.

Arrested in November 1989 immediately after the regime changed hands, a mockery of a trial in 1990 found Zhivkov guilty of embezzlement and, though he was sentenced to life imprisonment, he spent the years until his death in 1998 under comfortable house arrest.

Vitosha

The presence of the Vitosha Mountains just 10km (6 miles) from the centre of the city makes Sofia one of the most fortunate capitals in Europe. Access to **Vitosha National Park** (Национален Парк Витоша) from Sofia is easy: a taxi will cost no more than 10 leva to either the **Dragalevtsi chair lift** or **Simeonovo gondola** stations. Public transport to both is surprisingly unreliable outside the ski season (December to April).

Dragalevtsi (Драгалевци), a charming village offering a number of good places to stay and eat, is most famous for its **monastery**, built in the mid-14th century. Though little of the monastery remains, the original 14th-century church and a few of the original cloisters – one of which sheltered revolutionary Vasil Levski from the Ottoman secret police in the 1860s – are in good condition, while the gladed setting alone is well worth the 15-minute walk up from the chairlift station. **Simeonovo** (Симеоново) is a less interesting village, notable only for its access to Vitosha via its gondola, which is quicker than the Dragalevtsi chairlift, and during winter queues here are shorter.

Both the Dragalevtsi and Simeonovo lifts terminate at **Aleko** (Алеко), the heart of Vitosha, at an altitude of 2,000m (6,560ft). From here a small number of chair and drag lifts radiate out to form a half-decent ski area in winter, though advanced skiers will be bored in a day or two as there are few difficult pistes around Aleko. The hotels up here all rent out ski equipment and can arrange for instruction. Aleko is swamped by Sofians every winter weekend, so it's best to ski from Monday to Friday. The spring, summer and autumn are different stories entirely. The chairlifts usually operate only at weekends, but with locals usually preferring to walk the well- marked paths, you should never have to wait too long. The tallest peak in the range, **Cerni Vrah** at 2,290m (7,515ft), can be scaled by the fit in an hour's hike from Aleko.

Striking Iskar Gorge

DAY TRIPS FROM SOFIA

There are a number of worthwhile attractions in the vicinity of Sofia, but they are scattered to all points of the compass at varying distances from the city. The best solution if you wish to explore the area is to stay in the capital and hire a car, perhaps combining two or three destinations in a day if they are in the same general direction.

North of Sofia

There are several routes leading north from the capital. The most striking follows the 156km (97-mile) **Iskar Gorge**. Narrow and bumpy in places, it is rarely busy, and there are plenty of places to pull over along the way to admire the views. The most stunning parts of the gorge are between **Novi Iskar** and **Lyutibrod**, an area that was almost completely cut off from the rest of Bulgaria until the railway was built in the 1890s. The road came much later. Even today the only settlement of any size is **Svoge**, situated in one of the remotest and most spectacular parts of the gorge, where the Iskar and Iskrets rivers meet.

The mountains north of Sofia have the greatest concentration of **monasteries** in the country. The most accessible is the **Cherepish Monastery**, which is located close to where the Iskar Gorge peters out around Lyutibrad. Legend has it that in the 14th century Tsar Ivan Shishman fought and defeated an unnamed enemy here – probably the Turks – before beheading the dead and burying their skulls on the site where the monastery was built shortly afterwards. Locals insist that the very name of the monastery (*cherep* means 'scalp' in Bulgarian) attests to the truth of the myth. Today, the monastery is known more for its 15th-century gospel bound with gold covers and its Festival of the Assumption on 15 August, when it is swamped by large numbers of day-trippers from Sofia.

Hristo Botev

The poet Hristo Botev, the most romantic of all Bulgaria's revolutionaries, was born in Kalofer, near Kazanlak, in 1848 – Europe's year of revolutions. Exiled to Romania in 1867, after provoking the wrath of the Turkish authorities with his nationalist public speaking, Botev threw himself into literary pursuits, acting as an editor of a number of émigré newspapers, as well as writing increasingly nationalistic poetry. He became de facto leader of the Bulgarian Revolutionary Committee in 1873 after Vasil Levski's execution, and presided from afar over the disastrous April Revolt of 1876. After the revolt had been crushed, Botev, with 200 supporters, attempted to galvanise Bulgaria's nationalists in support of a new revolt, only to be killed on 20 May by a Turkish patrol while making his way to the town of Vratsa. His 1875 volume, *Songs and Poems*, remains the finest work of Bulgarian national poetry.

More off the beaten track is the **Sedemte Prestola Monastery**, which lies nestled in wooded hills about 15km (9 miles) along the side valley of the Gabrovnitsa stream (turn off the main gorge route at Eliseina). Built in the 11th century, destroyed and rebuilt in the 18th, the monastery was always a popular refuge for outlaws, bandits and nationalists.

Fresco in Cherepish Monastery

Further north is the small town of **Vratsa** (Враца), gateway to **Vratsa Gorge**, which begins just 2km (1½ miles) beyond the city centre and is an excellent day-trip on its own. There are two good museums to visit, the **Ethnographical Museum** and the **History Museum** (both open Tues–Sun 9am–noon, 2–5pm; admission fee). The Ethnographical Museum has a number of Revival-period houses, and a large warehouse displaying 19th-century Orazov horse-drawn carriages. The History Museum's highlight is the peerless **Rogozen treasure**, a stash of silver found in 1985 in nearby Rogozen village, dating from the 5th century BC.

The only other town of note further north is **Berkovitsa**, once famous for its pottery but now not really worth a visit, though a small **Ethnographic Museum** does try to keep the city's heritage alive.

East of Sofia

Known to all Bulgarian schoolchildren as the cradle of the modern Bulgarian state, **Koprovshtitsa** (Копривщица), 75km (47 miles) east of Sofia, was the site of the ill-fated April Rising of

1876, when a rudimentary force of Bulgarian nationalists sought to spark a nationwide revolt that would finally free Bulgaria from the Turks. Though the rising was ruthlessly suppressed, it did at least raise international awareness of the brutality of the Turkish regime in Bulgaria, and the town has remained a symbol of Bulgarian nationalism and culture. For such reasons it is the host of a national music festival (held every five years, it is next due in August 2010). At an altitude of 1,060m (3,480ft), the town is also a popular mountain resort.

The primary attractions of Koprovshtitsa, however, are its **National Revival-period houses**, six of which are open to the public as museums. You can buy a ticket (12 leva) valid for entry to all six museums from the Museum Administration Office (open Mon–Sat 10.30am–6.30pm, tel: 07184 2180). English-language guided tours of the houses are also available, though you should phone ahead to check.

A rich merchant once owned this house in Koprovshtitsa

West of Sofia

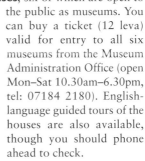

Pernik (Перник), 25km (15 miles) west of Sofia, is one of the best places in Bulgaria to witness the bizarre **Kukeri festivals** *(see page 94)* for which the country is famed. Over the last weekend of January thousands of men dress in costumes usually made of dead animals – including the heads – designed to evoke fear and scare off evil spirits. Dressed like this, they then spend long hours in a trance-like state dancing and chanting throughout the town. The origins of Kukeri are vague, but the practice is thought to have derived from the religions of the ancient Thracians.

Beyond Pernik, following the same road to Kyustendil, **Zemen Monastery** has Bulgaria's best collection of 14th-century frescoes, restored to greatness in the 1970s. The exterior of the monastery is not as lavish as others in Bulgaria and its position, on a hill hidden from the town of Zemen (Земен), is one of the most secluded. The meandering Struma river flows through the scenic 25-km (15-mile) long **Zemen Gorge**; however, the road skirts around the gorge so the only access is on foot (though the railway line does pass through it). The 70-m (240-ft) high **Skakavitza waterfall** near the village of Kamenishka Skakavitza is just one of the highlights.

Zemen Monastery

THE PIRIN AND RILA MOUNTAINS

Directly south of Sofia is the small Rila mountain range, known primarily for the Rila Monastery, Bulgaria's most famous attraction. Further south, stretching towards Greece, are the Pirin Mountains. Both ranges offer decent skiing (at Borovets in the Rila, at Bansko in the Pirin) and serve as good bases for hiking and walking, especially from the spa town of Sandanski.

Detail from the Church of the Annunciation, Blagoevgrad

Blagoevgrad

The largest city in the south-west of the country, **Blagoevgrad** (Благоевград) has a population of around 75,000 and sits at the foot of the Rila Mountains on the banks of the Blagoevgradaksa Bistritsa River. A major spa resort since the 16th century, it has 30 hot springs, some with temperatures of up to 55°C (130°F). A centre of learning since the Rila monks set up a university in the 17th century, it today plays host to four universities and thousands of students who swell the population during term time. Though devoid of real attractions, apart from the fine **History Museum** (open Mon–Sat 9am–noon, 1–5.30pm; admission fee), Blagoevgrad is a worthy stopping-off point for its cultural mix and access to more interesting parts of the region.

With its annual influx of budding young minds, Blagoevgrad is one of the major cultural centres of Bulgaria. The city supports a chamber opera noted throughout the country, as well as the Pirin Folk Ensemble, Bugaria's most popular folk music combo, which can be seen on stage at the American University when not on tour.

Out of town at Stob, a short bus journey from Blagoevgrad on the route to the Rila Monastery, are wierdly shaped natural red rock formations known as the **Stob pyramids**. A well signposted path and set of steps from the main road makes access to the pyramids straightforward. The **Bachinovo Park**, just north of the town, is a favourite hiking venue, while further along the same valley is **Bodrost**, a spa resort and hiking centre that allows access to the **Parangalitsa** nature reserve and the ancient fortress of **Klissoura**.

South of Blagoevgrad

Close to the Greek border, **Sandanski** (Сандански) is another spa town, set in the Pirin foothills at an altitude of 240m (787ft). Named after Yane Sandanski, a Macedonian rebel who fought against the Turks, it is located on the site of an old Thracian settlement that made good use of the springs. The Romans built a huge public bath complex, the Askelpion, and the town flourished until the 6th century when it was destroyed and fell into decay. When Bulgaria was fully liberated from Turkey in 1912, the town had a population of around 500. Today it is home to 25,000. The town's large **public bath complex** remains very popular and is well worth a day's bathing. Find it behind the cruise-ship-shaped Hotel Sandanski.

Sandstone pinnacle, Melnik

To the southeast of Sandanski is **Melnik** (Мелник), a living museum set gloriously amid steep slopes and crags. Once populated almost exclusively by Greeks, the town is now virtually deserted, having never recovered after being largely destroyed during the Balkan Wars of

1912–13. There remains, however, much to see. A number of Revival-period houses can be visited (opening times vary; admission fee), while to the south of the town above the river, on the **Nikolova Gora** – about 30 minutes' walk uphill – are the **Sv Nikola Church** and the fearsome remains of a **Slav fortress**. The views of the town below are stunning.

Melnik is also the gateway to **Rozhen Monastery**, which is 6km (4 miles) further on and accessible by bus. The original 13th-century monastery was burnt down; the current structure dates from the 17th century. Most visitors prefer to walk, however, either along the road or by two mountain routes – one taking about two hours, the other three hours; both are well signposted from Melnik. The road is popular because it passes some of Bulgaria's most spectacular **sandstone pyramids**, several more than 80m (260ft) tall, cut over thousands of years by the Melnik and Rozhen rivers, with rain doing the rest of the sculptural work. Most are not pyramids at all, but various odd-looking shapes.

It doesn't have to be winter to enjoy the ice in Bansko

Bansko

Currently the most fashionable resort in the Balkans, **Bansko** (Банско) is showing serious signs of over development. Until 2003 skiers in Bansko had to take a 40 minute bus ride to the ski area, but that winter saw the opening of a fast gondola lift direct to the ski area. This was followed by a massive boom in construction, causing the small, sleepy National Revival-era town to almost double in size. Smart hotel and apartment complexes now dot the suburbs, and many have been built without thought for the surroundings. Investment in the ski area has not kept pace with construction, and weekend lift queues,

Bansko's town sign

unheard of just a few years ago, are now as long as anywhere else in the country. But snow remains guaranteed (almost all the slopes are above 1,400m/4,600ft; the town itself sits at 925m/3,035ft), and mid-week skiing can be blissful.

There is far more to Bansko than skiing; the town has been a popular destination for many years. Its cobbled streets are lined with fine houses, many of which date from the beginning of the 19th century when the town was an important trading centre on the overland route from the Middle East to the Aegean Sea. Bansko grew rich on the back of commerce, and grand houses, churches, schools and cultural buildings sprang up apace. Although the town's prosperity suffered towards the end of the century, when the Danube was opened to traffic and the trade route ceased, Bansko was revived in the early 20th century as a weekend holiday destination for Sofians.

Even the planners of the socialist era preserved the atmosphere of Bansko, and the modern areas of the city around the central square, **pl Nikola Vaptsarov** – named after Nikola

Freedom fighters monument
in Vazrazhdane Square

Vaptsarov, a revolutionary poet – blend with the old. The most notable sights in Bansko are centred on the older **pl Vazrazhdane**. The **Church of Sv Troitsa** is the largest in the region and was completed in 1835, when Bansko's prosperity was at its height. Large does not always translate as enthralling, however, and the outside of the church is rather bland. The interior is much more interesting, with icons painted by Dimitar Molerov, a leading figure in the Bansko School of Art that flourished at the same time as the town. The **stone tower** in the courtyard was added 30 years after the church had been completed.

Anyone with an interest in Bulgarian culture or history might like to visit the **Neofit Rilski House Museum** (open daily 9am–noon, 2–6pm; admission fee), located behind the church at ul Pirin 17. This was the childhood home of Neofit Rilski, a leading member in the Bulgarian cultural revival of the 19th century, who, among other achievements, was a member of the scholarly collective that first translated the New Testament into Bulgarian. The house has been preserved to retain its original appearance; inside photographs explain Rilski's career. The **Icon Museum** (open daily 9am–noon, 2–6pm; admission fee) in the **Rilski Convent**, on the other side of pl Vazrazhdane, is another gem, showcasing the works of Dimitar Molerov and his contemporaries, who produced countless masterpieces for the merchants of the town who patronised the Bansko School.

Rila Monastery

Northeast of Blagoevgrad lies the Rila range, and Bulgaria's most visited attraction: Rila Monastery. The Rila range is the sixth-highest in Europe and the Moussala, at 2,925m (9,600ft), is the highest mountain in the Balkans. The range is home to thousands of small lakes. Samokov is the region's main town.

Among the peaks, valleys, lakes and forests lies the world-famous **Rila Monastery** (Рилски Манастир; open daily summer 7am–8pm, winter 8am–5pm), an outstanding example of National Revival-period architecture. It can be seen in a rushed day-trip from Sofia, but a more leisurely visit is recommended, with tours departing from Borovets, Bansko and Blagoevgrad almost every day of the year. There is a regular bus service to the monastery from Blagoevgrad, Dupnitsa and the small village of Rila. Independent travellers with cars can drive to the monastery from Blagoevgrad in about an hour.

Church of the Virgin Birth, Rila Monastery

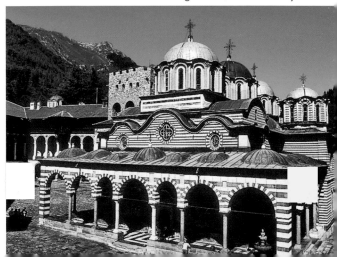

The Rafail Cross

A unique specimen of the art of woodcarving, the Rafail Cross in Rila Monastery is made of a whole piece of wood 81cm x 43cm (32in x 17in) in size. It was made in the latter half of the 18th century by a Rila monk, Rafail, who took 12 years to complete it. Interwoven in the miniature woodcarving are no less than 104 religious scenes and 650 small figures: the largest carving is no bigger than a grain of rice. Rafail used fine chisels, small knives and a magnifying glass in his work, and all but lost his sight as a result.

A monastery has stood on this site since St John of Rila (Sveti Ivan Rilski, patron saint of Bulgaria) founded one in the 10th century, but the current structure dates from 1816–47, the original having been all but destroyed by the Turks in the 18th century. The East Wing Museum was completed in 1961.

From the outside the monastery looks like a medieval fortress, and the wonders of the interior are a hidden delight. The most spectacular of the monastery buildings is the **Church of the Virgin Birth**, with sublime porticos and colonnades. Inside the church, the elaborate icons and use of gold leaf betray the wealth of the monastery builders and the power that the region once had. The **Hand of St John of Rila**, a relic of the saint, is kept inside the church, though it is rarely on display. Another treasure is the 12th-century **Icon of the Virgin**, which can usually only be seen on Assumption Day, 15 August.

The elegant **Tower of Hreylo** looms large beside the church, and is the only part of the original monastery that survives. The **Preobrazhenie Chapel** on the top floor houses a fine museum of 14th-century murals. Most of the original treasures of the monastery are now housed in the **East Wing Museum** (admission fee), including the doors of the Hrelyo Church, icons and the beautiful **Rafail Cross** (see box, above).

Something resembling an entire village has now grown up around the monastery to serve the tourists and pilgrims who visit it all year round, including two hotels, the Tsarev Vruh and the Rilets, of which the latter is easily preferable. The monastery also offers the most basic of accommodation in its dormitories.

Borovets

The largest of Bulgaria's ski resorts, **Borovets** (Боровец) has been playing host to visitors since the mayor of nearby Samokov built a chalet here for his wife in the 1890s to alleviate her tuberculosis; other wealthy families – including the tsar's – quickly followed suit. The resort remained an exclusive hideaway of the rich until the 1950s, when the Communist authorities developed it primarily for the use of party members. The idea of investing heavily in hotels and ski lifts to attract

Rila Hotel complex, Borovets

foreign cash was a 1960s' afterthought. Since then the resort has seen massive development and is today dominated by two enormous hotels, the Rila and the Samokov, almost self-contained resorts in themselves. From the Rila a network of chairlifts and drag lifts branch out to form one of the ski areas, known as the **Sitnyakovo**, while a fast gondola lift takes skiers up to the second ski area, the **Yastrabets**, from its terminus just beside the Samokov. In all there are around 55km (35 miles) of piste in Borovets, some of it quite challenging. Snow is reliable from late December to the end of March.

Once the snow has gone, skiers give way to hikers, but this is not the best walking country in Bulgaria. The most interesting and, for the fit, challenging is the walk up to Yastrabets, which takes a good five hours, and from there onwards to the peak of Moussala is another hour and a half.

Wherever you stay in Borovets, be it the Samokov or the simple Malina Chalets, prices are always cheaper as part of a package tour. Turning up on spec can be expensive, and at weekends during the high season (February and Easter) risky, as the resort can be full.

PLOVDIV & THE RHODOPE MOUNTAINS

Plovdiv, in the Plain of Thrace, is the country's second-largest city, and perhaps the most picturesque. The Rhodopes, which spread out from the plain in a generally southerly direction, are a meandering range of mountains that offer good hiking and walking. There is skiing, too, at Chepelare and Pamporovo.

Philip of Macedonia founded **Plovdiv** (Пловдив) in 342BC, and named the town Philipopolis after himself. For centuries it was little more than a garrison town, until the Romans developed its potential as a trading halt on the route from Constantinople to Belgrade. Known to the Romans as Trimontium, Plovdiv today has a population of almost

400,000. It is a genuine rival to Sofia in terms of historical importance, and though a Sofian would baulk at the suggestion, given the variety of good hotels, cafés, bars, restaurants, its vibrant cultural scene and access to the Rhodopes, Plovdiv may indeed be a finer place to spend a few days than the capital itself.

Downtown Plovdiv

The centre of modern Plovdiv is the megalithic **pl Tsentralen**, a public square too big for itself and the town, dominated by the Trimontium Princess Hotel, one of the city's best. Remains of the **Roman Forum** were discovered when the square was built, and are now preserved in an area next to the post office. The west of the square is bordered by the **Tsar Simeon Park**, a well-kept but attraction-free garden, popular with courting teenagers.

Imposing Trimontium Princess Hotel in Plovdiv's central square

Plovdiv's 2nd-century Roman Amphitheatre

Leading directly northwards from pl Tsentralen is the pedestrianised **Alexander I Boulevard**, the major shopping street. The **Plovdiv City Art Gallery** (open Mon–Fri 9am–5pm) here is disappointing, while on the left-hand side the often rebuilt Clock Tower stands forlornly on top of Sahat Tepe, one of the city's hills.

Bul Alexander I is the best way to reach the splendid **Roman Amphitheatre** (turn right at ul Dospevski and head up the hill; open daily 9am–5pm), built during the reign of Emperor Marcus Aurelius in the 2nd century AD and the best preserved Roman monument in Bulgaria. It is now used as a venue for operas, plays and concerts almost every evening throughout the summer, most notably the annual **Verdi Festival**, usually held during the first week of July.

At its northern end, bul Alexander I reaches **pl Dzhumaya**, a microcosm of Bulgarian history, containing the less-than-impressive ruins of a **Roman Stadium** and one of the most stunning mosques in the country, the **Dzhumaya Dzhamiya** (open daily except Fri). One of 53 mosques erected by the Turks in Plovdiv during their 500-year rule of the city, the Dzamiya was built in the 14th century, during the reign of Murad II (1359–85). It is a towering construction, its thick, high walls and 25-m (82-ft) high minaret dominating the surrounding area.

Old Town

The best way to enter Plovdiv's **Old Town** is to follow ul Saborna, which meanders uphill to the Nebet Tepe Citadel from pl Dzhumaya. The first sight that looms on the right is the **Church of the Virgin Mary** (open daily 7.30am–7pm) with a strikingly colourful pink and blue loggia. Further along on the right the visitor passes the small **Gallery of Fine Arts** (open Mon–Sat 9am–5.30pm; admission fee) and the **Apteka Hipokrat** (open daily 10am–5pm; admission fee), a fascinating – but again small – pharmaceutical museum. Next comes the **House of Zlatyu Boyadzhiev** at No. 18 (open Mon–Fri 9am–5pm), a gallery dedicated to Zlatyu Boyadzhiev, a talented modern painter whose reputation is tainted by his one-time willingness to please the Communist Party with socialist-realist works depicting idealised, happy peasants. Two doors further along is the **Icon Museum** (open daily 9am–12.30pm, 1.30–5pm; admission fee) packed to the rafters with religious art from the surrounding region, while next door is the **Church of Ss Konstantin i Elena**, the oldest Christian church in Plovdiv, built on what was the wall of the original Macedonian fortress. Some of the icons inside date from the 14th century, though master iconographer Zahari Zograf added many during the National Revival in the 19th century. Next to the church stands the **Hisar Kapiya**, the eastern gate of the Macedonian fortress, though little of the gate we see today is original.

From the gate, carry on up the ever steeper hill towards the shabby ruins of the **Nebet Tepe Citadel**. Plovdiv's stunning **Ethnographical Museum** (open Mon and Fri 2–5pm, Tues–Thur and Sat–Sun 9am–noon, 2–5pm; admission fee) is on the right, at ul Chomarov 2. Set in the former house of Greek merchant Argir Koyumdzhioglou, the museum collection is good, but it is the house (dating from the 1840s) and gardens that people come to see. Chamber concerts are performed in the gardens in the summer, most notably in June when the annual **Plovdiv International Chamber Music Festival** is held here.

Passing back under the Hisar Kapiya, you reach the ornate **Museum of National Liberation** (open Tues–Sun 9am– noon, 2–5pm) in the former home of a wealthy Turkish merchant. The museum is an excellent primer on the Bulgarian National Revival and struggle for liberation, with many exhibits carrying English captions.

South of Plovdiv – the Central Rhodopes

Assenovgrad, the first town south of Plovdiv, is famed for its vineyards, but there is little here to keep you, apart from the medieval fortress, a short distance outside of town on the road to Smolyan, and the Bachkovo Monastery, second only to Rila among Bulgaria's finest religious buildings.

The **Fortress of Assenovgrad (Assenova Krepost)** has a fabled history of command and conquest, though its remains today are less than worthy of its past. The steep rocky hillside is a perfect position to guard the access to

Climbing up to the Fortress of Assenovgrad

Bachkovo Monastery

the Plain of Thrace and it was first used as a defensive bulwark by the Thracians, though the first substantial fortress was built during the reign of Tsar Ivan Assen II in the 13th century. The best preserved part is the **Petrich Church of the Virgin Mary** (open Wed–Sun 8am–5pm; admission fee), dominating the site.

Founded in 1083 by a Byzantine statesman of Georgian origin, the **Bachkovo Monastery** (Бачковоски манастир; open daily 7am–9pm, guides available 10am–4pm), 11km (7 miles) south of Assenovgrad, is a fine collection of well-preserved historic buildings from various eras. Highlights are the **refectory**, with frescoed walls depicting the monastery's history, and two churches, the Sv Nikolai and the Church of the Virgin Mary, the oldest building in the monastery, dating from 1604. The Church of the Virgin Mary houses the **Icon of the Virgin**, supposed to have been brought from Georgia in 1310. Every year on Assumption Day, 15 August, it is paraded by thousands of pilgrims in a procession around the monastery.

Chepelare and Pamporovo

A new chair-lift has revolutionised the previously limited ski-ing at **Chepelare**, which looks set to become the country's next boom resort. But most visitors to this region still make a bee-line for **Pamporovo** (Пампорово), the most developed of Bulgaria's ski resorts. A great choice for families, it is far more suited to beginners than other Bulgarian resorts. The gentle slopes make for easy skiing (there is, however, one short black run called 'the Wall', which is recognised as the toughest piste in the country), and the ski-school is excellent. While it offers a great choice of hotels, Pamporovo has nevertheless resisted the temptation to expand bed capacity too much. Lift queues here are significantly shorter here, even at weekends. During the summer Pamporovo is all but deserted, and makes a peaceful destination for gentle walks and fine air.

The Western Rhodopes

Heading west from Pamporovo – with a car preferably, as public transport in this remote part of Bulgaria is often non-existent – you enter an area populated almost entirely by a people known as the Pomaks, Bulgarians converted to Islam by the Turks in the 17th century. Though the occasional

Bears

Bulgaria is home to approximately 750 brown bears, one of the largest populations in Europe. The majority live in the Rila and Rhodope mountains at an altitude of around 1,100m (3,600ft). Small numbers are hunted each year, though these are usually problem bears identified by the authorities as dangerous to the overall well-being of a group. The high charges paid by hunters also help to fund conservation programmes. Contact with people is extremely rare (about 150 cases each year), of which about a third end with bears attacking humans.

Christian village is dotted here and there, mosques, many brand new, dominate the landscape.

Cobbled street in Shiroka Luka

Shiroka Luka (Широка Лька), a short distance from Pamporovo, is a village museum often full of package tourists from Pamporovo trying to get a feel of the real Bulgaria. Though short on individual attractions, apart from the **Church of the Assumption** which has Zograf frescoes, the village is a delight to amble around, with cobbled streets, large Rhodope houses and picturesque courtyards. It is also a great place to witness the **Kukeri festival**, which takes place each year on the first Sunday of March.

Passing through the spa town of **Devin** (Девин), most visitors head straight for the **Trigad Gorge**, a steep, narrow chasm cut by the lively River Trogradska. At the apex of the gorge the river plunges down into a cave known as the **Dyavolskoto Gurlo** or **Devil's Throat** (open Wed–Sun; guided tours only; admission fee discretional), one of the most spectacular natural sights in the country. A viewing platform has been positioned over the point where the river goes underground, while the tour of the cave, which is memorable for its sheer size and deafening echo of gushing water, is not for the faint-hearted. The village of **Trigrad** (Триград) has little to recommend it, but it has a couple of good hotels that

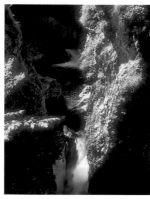

The spectacular Devil's Throat at the apex of the Trigrad Gorge

make it a popular base for hiking and caving. The neighbouring village of **Yagodina** (Ягодина) is a major centre for Bulgarian caving.

A short drive or a long hike from Trigrad, heading back towards Devin and turning right shortly before the gorge, is the village of **Mugla**, which wouldn't figure on any map were it not for the annual **gaidi (bagpipe) festival** that takes place here each August.

The Eastern Rhodopes

The remote **Eastern Rhodopes** are best accessed via **Dimitrovgrad**, an hour's drive from Plovdiv. Along with Kraków's suburb of Nowa Huta in Poland, Dimitrovgrad shares the distinction of being an entirely planned Socialist-Realist city. Built in the 1950s, its wide boulevards and monumental apartments blocks are potholed and faded today, but the scale is a testament to the belief once placed in Communism.

Heading south into the mountains the pink **Kardzhali pyramids** greet visitors to the town of the same name. Just one of many weird rock formations in the once volcanic area, the pyramids (also known as the Svatba Vkame-nenata, or Stone Wedding) are said by locals to be a wedding party turned to stone by the gods to punish the bridegroom's mother for envying the bride's beauty. **Kardzahli** is a nice enough town, but the only real sight is the **ruined fortress of Perperikon**, 20km (13 miles) northeast of town, where archaeologists have unearthed layers of civilisation going back some 7,000 years.

THE EASTERN BALKANS

Characterised by magnificent scenery and endless historical tales of heroism, liberation and derring-do, the Eastern Balkans form what is often described as both the cradle and the nursery of the Bulgarian nation. The magnificent fortress at Veliko Tarnovo defended one of the largest cities in medieval Europe when it was capital of the Second Bulgarian Kingdom; monasteries were built in abundance – there are more than 40 in the region – and the largely unspoiled area remains today a symbol of national pride and togetherness.

Veliko Tarnovo

The majestic capital of the Second Bulgarian Kingdom, **Veliko Tarnovo** (Велико Търново) is one of the most picturesque cities in Bulgaria, mainly due to its setting on the steep banks of the Yantra River. Offering a good choice of accommodation, it is an excellent base from which to explore the historically significant surrounding area. The exquisite village of Arbanassi is close by, as is the Preobrazhenski Monastery, the finest and best preserved in the region.

At various times called Ternov, Trunov, Turnovgrad or simply Tarnovo, Veliko Tarnovo's existence has long

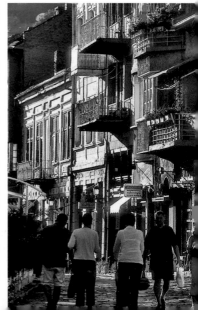

Veliko Tarnovo's tranquil Old Town

Tsaravets fortress, cradle of the nation

depended on possession of the imposing citadel that sits atop
Tsaravets, the highest of the three sacred hills among which
the city nestles. The main attraction in Veliko Tarnovo, Tsaravets (open daily Apr–Sept 8am–7pm, Oct–Mar 10am–5pm;
admission fee) was first settled by the Thracians, though the
first fortifications were probably constructed by the Byzantines
in the 6th and 7th centuries. As the Byzantine Empire declined,
that first fortress fell into ruins, which were built on in the 10th
century by the Slavs, who were responsible for much of the
structure that can be seen today. By the 12th century, the city
was densely populated. Its position as the cradle of the nation
was set in stone in 1187, when the successful rebellion of Peter
and Assen against Byzantium was launched from Tsaravets,
and Peter proclaimed a new Bulgarian Kingdom. Over the next
200 years the town flourished, until the summer of 1393 when,
after a three-month siege, the overwhelmingly powerful Turkish army overran the citadel and set the town alight.

What remains of the fortress today is dominated by its restored **southern ramparts** and **Baldwin's Tower**, while the **Bulgarian Patriarchate**, with a rather orange exterior and green domes, towers above the ruins of the Tsar's Palace, which only hint at the size it must once have been.

A number of other churches surround the Tsaravets, the best preserved being the **Church of Peter and Paul** – at the foot of Tsaravet's northern slopes where the Yantra performs one of its many U-turns – and the **Church of the 40 Martyrs**, slightly further along Mitropolska towards Old Town.

Veliko Tarnovo's **Old Town** can become crowded with day-trippers, but it's usually a relaxed, even sleepy place, perfect for exploring on foot. Unfortunately, the three **museums** (**Archaelogical, National Revival** and **History**; all open daily 9am–noon, 2–5pm; admission fee) in the centre fail to understand that non-Bulgarians may also be interested in the country's history; all captions are in Bulgarian only and there are no guided tours.

From the Old Town, most visitors make their way up ul Jamiyata, which leads to pl Velchova Zavera and the **House of the Monkey**, so called because a tiny monkey statue sits below the first-floor bay window. The market in **pl Samodivska**, behind pl Velchova Zavera, is one of the best places in Bulgaria to find handmade pottery *(see pages 89–90)*.

From here begins **ul Stamboliski**, the city's primary commercial street, with shops, cafés and restaurants, a number of which have small terraces at the back that offer great views of the valley below. The **monument** in **pl Pobornicheski** marks the site where revolutionaries Bacho Kiro, Tsanko Dyustabanov and Georgi Izmirliev were hanged by the Turks in 1876. More shops, cafés and restaurants line the route towards **pl Nezavisimost**, the centre of modern Veliko Tarnovo.

The huge, orange building that dominates the lower part of Veliko Tarnovo is the **Boris Denev Art Gallery** (open Tues–

Sat 10am–6pm). The awful monument in front of it is a tribute to the Assen Dynasty, put up in the 1980s as part of the 1,300 years of Bulgaria celebrations. Surrounding the art gallery is a shaded park with gentle paths perfect for afternoon strolls.

Around Veliko Tarnovo

The village-museum of **Arbanasi** (Арбанаси), a 10-minute drive uphill from Veliko Tarnovo, has more charms per square kilometre than any other village in Bulgaria. A flourishing trade and craft centre from the middle of the 16th century, the village is made up of monumental fortress-style houses and exquisite churches. The best of these is the **Church of the Archangels Michael and Gabriel** (admission fee) on a small hill above the village's park, and the **Kostantsialev House** (open daily 10am–noon, 2–5pm; admission fee) on the other side of the park. In all, there are five house-museums and four churches, as well as two rather plain monasteries.

Returning to Veliko Tarnovo and taking the main road for Ruse, the **Preobrazhensk Monastery** is situated about 6km (4 miles) north of the town. One of many monasteries in the area founded in the 14th century, it flourished during the Second Bulgarian Kingdom only to be burnt by the Turks after they had taken Veliko Tarnovo. Rebuilt in the 19th century during the National Revival, it is a fine example of the era's architecture and iconography. The central **Church of the Transfiguration** includes two characteristic frescoes by Zahari Zograf, the *Last*

Souvenir dolls from the Kostantsialev House

Preobrazhensk Monastery

Judgement and the *Wheel of Life*. There are two other churches in the monastery, the **Church of the Annunciation**, with icons by Stanislav Dospevski, and the **Church of the Ascension**. The **bell** in the courtyard's bell tower was a gift from Russia's Tsar Alexander II.

South of Veliko Tarnovo is the equally remarkable **Kilifarevo Monastery**. Founded by Teodisil Turnovski as a centre of Hesychasm, a religious doctrine that preached unity with God through isolation, it was another monastery burnt to the ground by the Turks in the late 14th century, only to be refounded and rebuilt in the 19th century. It's impressive central church, the **Church of Sv Dimitar**, includes a stunning portrait of St John of Rila by Kristu Zahariev.

South of Veliko Tarnovo

Southwest of Veliko Tarnovo towards Kazanlak is the small town of **Dryanovo** (Дряново), another town associated with rebellion and nationalism. Dating back to the 12th century, the town's **Monastery**, 4km (2 miles) further on, was the sight of an anti-Turkish uprising in 1876, when 220 revolutionaries led by Bacho Kiro held a large Turkish army at bay for nine days before the Turks blew the monastery up and hanged the rebels in Veliko Tarnovo. Most of the monastery's buildings were fully restored after liberation. Just beyond the monastery is the floodlit **Bacho Kiro Cave** (open daily during the summer, irregular hours), a good opportunity to see stalactites and stalagmites.

Climbing steadily into the Balkans, **Gabrovo** (Габрово), gateway to the Shipka Pass, is a former textile town with little to

The legendary Shipka Pass

offer except its **Museum of Humour and Satire** (ul Bryanska 64, open Tues–Sun 9am–6pm; admission fee) and the **International Biennial of Humour and Satire** (in May in odd-numbered years). The museum and festival are in Gabrovo because it is the traditional butt of most Bulgarian jokes, usually involving meanness and stupidity. Some 8km (5 miles) southeast of the town is **Etura** (open daily 8am–6pm; admission fee), a craft centre set up to preserve the town's traditional skills. The complex's houses, workshops and mills recreate with astonishing realism what life was like in Gabrovo 150 years ago.

South of Gabrovo is the stunning **Shipka Pass**, equal in majesty to the Iskar Gorge and every bit as deserving of its legendary status among locals. It was here that Alexander the Great won one of his first major victories as Macedonian leader in 335BC and where – more importantly for Bulgarians – in August 1877 a Bulgarian and Russian force held back 30,000 Turks, thus allowing

An aquiline door handle on Shipka's Memorial to Freedom

Pleven to be taken by other Bulgarian and Russian forces. Today, at the 1,326m (4,350ft) summit of Mt Stoletov, you will find the **Memorial to Freedom**, which is accessible from the road by 894 steps. The memorial houses a small museum (open 9am–5pm) dedicated to the battle. Beyond the apex of the pass, the village of **Shipka** (Шипка) is home to the splendid, pink, white and golden-domed **Shipka Memorial Church**, built in 1902 to commemorate the battle.

Kazanlak and Stara Zagora

During the first weekend of June each year, the town of **Kazanlak** (Казанлък) holds the **Festival of the Roses**, an ages-old pageant celebrating the rose harvest of the surrounding villages, which together form what Bulgarians refer to as the **Valley of the Roses**. The roses are in full bloom during the late spring. Kazanlak became rich on its rose oil during the 18th century, and today the **Museum of the Rose** (open daily 9am–5.30pm; admission fee) in Tyubelto Park tells the story.

The biggest draw in town, however, is the **Thracian Tomb** (open daily 9am–5pm; admission fee), also in Tyubelto Park, dating from the 4th century BC and excavated in 1944. So precious is Bulgaria's finest surviving example of Thracian art that the tomb is closed to the public. The replica next to it is a perfect reproduction of the original in every respect, from the red floors to the stunning frescoes on the domed ceiling.

Situated in the geographical centre of Bulgaria, **Stara Zagora** (Стара Загора) is one of the country's largest cities. Founded as Beroe in the 6th century BC by the Thracians it became the Roman town Augusta Traiana, the Byzantine town Irinopolis and the Turkish town Eski Zaara, before being completely destroyed by the Turks during the war of liberation. After independence it was rebuilt following a grid system devised by the Czech urban planner Lubor Bayer. As with most planned towns, Stara Zagora lacks character and has little to offer the visitor except the **Bereketska Mogila Neolithic Dwellings**, the largest prehistoric settlement unearthed in Bulgaria. The dwellings (open Tues–Sun 9am–noon, 2–5pm; admission fee; English guided tours) date from at least 5500BC and provide a fascinating insight into the life of the ancient people who lived in them.

Rose Oil

Bulgaria has been one of the world's leading producers of rose oil since the 18th century, when Turkish traders noticed that the area around Kazanlak (now known as the Valley of the Roses) would be perfect for cultivating the flower. Harvesting the rose is a race against time, as the flower must be picked before 9am, when it is still wet with dew. The harvest must then be rushed to the distillery before the oil has evaporated. Bulgarian steam-distilled rose oil, 100 percent pure, is today recognised as being the finest – and most expensive – in the world, and is used in the production of perfumes, as well as in meditation. The Festival of the Roses is celebrated every June in Kazanlak.

Golden Sands, best known of Bulgaria's Black Sea beach resorts

THE BLACK SEA

Of all Bulgaria's charms as a holiday destination, it is the fantastic beaches and warm waters of the Black Sea that have been attracting tourists the longest. From brash Sunny Beach to chic Albena, from enchanting Balchick to bewitching Nessebur, Bulgaria's 400km (249 miles) of coastline offers everything: golden sands, rocky coves, nature reserves and delightful fishing villages. The region can be rough around the edges: the transport infrastructure (particularly the roads) is poor, customer service can be under par, and many resorts are blighted by construction sites. But for a great-value summer holiday there is nowhere in Europe to match Bulgaria's Black Sea coast. To get the best of it, spend a week or two at one of the many good hotels in the major beach resorts of Golden Sands or Sunny Beach, but don't neglect to visit the real gems: little Nessebur and ancient Sozopol.

Varna

The third-largest city in Bulgaria, **Varna** (Варна) is part sea-port and part beach resort. It has a mish-mash of cultures and architectural styles and a brashness that characterises most Black Sea towns and cities. Most of the thousands of tourists who come here on package tours head straight to the nearby resorts of Golden Sands and Albena, but Varna itself is definitely worth a look: a city of 350,000 that offers a vibrant café and restaurant scene, great museums, a rich cultural heritage and one of the finest operas in Bulgaria. It is also the best place to shop outside the capital. Like much of the Black Sea coast, however, Varna remains a little rough around the edges.

Varna's busy main square

Although there was once an ancient Thracian settlement close by, the city dates back to the 6th century BC, when Greek colonists founded the small settlement of Odessos, which quickly became an important centre of trade and fishing. Conquered in turn by Alexander the Great and the Romans, the city flourished under both of these empires until Barbarians destroyed it in 586. Repopulated by the Slavs, who gave the town its present name, Varna remained a city on the fringes until the 19th century when it became the most important seaport within the newly independent Bulgaria.

Pl Nezavisimost, Varna's pedestrianised central square, surrounded on all sides by terraces and cafés in the summer, is dominated by the shocking-pink, 19th-century **Varna Opera House and Philharmonia** and the **Old Clock Tower**, dating from 1880. Across the main boulevard, Hristo Botev, stands the 19th-century **Cathedral of the Holy Virgin**, more impressive from afar than it is close up. For though the interior is spectacular – the icons and frescoes took 25 years to complete – the exterior is in need of repair and you will be asked to make a donation, before being blessed, as you make your way inside. A good market selling local embroidery and lace besides the usual souvenirs surrounds the cathedral.

From here, a short walk along the pleasantly wide **Maria Luiza Boulevard** brings you to the **Varna Archaeological Museum** (open Tues–Sun 10am–6pm; admission fee), the city's best museum. Set in splendid gardens, it was built as a school during the National Revival. Various exhibits vie for your attention, including miniature models of Palaeolithic pile dwellings, ancient art and jewellery, and various ancient Egyptian, Greek and even Babylonian artefacts.

The awful skyscraper on the other side of the road is the Town Hall. Just north of here, on Rakovski Boulevard, is the Church of Sv Petka, famous for its striped walls and marvellous central cupola. To the south of the Town Hall is the **Art Gallery** (open Tues–Sun, 10am–6pm; admission fee), which houses a fine collection of Bulgarian and foreign art.

From the art gallery, it is a short walk to **Knyaz Boris I Boulevard**, the city's main thoroughfare and shopping street, which buzzes from morning until late at night throughout the summer. A short distance along this pedestrianised street is the **Sv Nikola Church**, which was built in 1866 and contains icons by many of the finest Bulgarian masters, though much of the church is inaccessible at present due to restoration

A town called Stalin

From 1947 until 1956 Varna was officially named Stalin in honour of the Soviet leader. A number of other cities in Eastern Europe, including Brasov in Romania, suffered a similar fate.

work. Just around the corner on ul 27 Yuli is the **National Revival Museum** (open Mon–Fri 10am–5pm; admission fee), a church and the Varna's first Bulgarian school before it became a museum in 1959. The story of the city's history and liberation is told, in English and Bulgarian, in well-preserved classrooms.

Heading towards the port along Han Krum, the **Church of Sv Bogodoritsa** looms on the left. This was built in the 17th century according to Turkish rules that limited the height of churches, hence it's sunken foundations and after-thought of a tower. On the other side of the road are the **Roman Thermae** (open Tues–Sat 10am–5pm; admission fee), built in the 2nd century and abandoned to the Barbarians in the 6th century. After much restoration work, the baths are now one of the city's most important archaeological sights. Almost adjacent to the Thermae is the **Church of Sv Atanasii**, a fine example of National Revival architecture. Another classic of the National Revival period houses the **Ethnographic Museum** (open Tues–Sun 10am–5.30pm; admission fee). Exhibits include various Kukeri masks, making this a good opportunity for travellers not fortunate enough to experience a Kukeri festival to see just how bizarre they are.

Primorski Park

The huge **Primorski Park**, stretching from Varna's port almost to the pleasant, tiny beach resort of **Sv Konstantin**, took years to lay out and was finally completed in 1908. Recently given a welcome facelift, it is very popular with locals, who flock here to sunbathe on Varna's excellent municipal **beach** or attend pop and rock concerts throughout the summer at the **open-air theatre**. The numerous terraces, pubs and discos lining the beachfront are full most nights all summer long.

The park has various attractions, some of dubious quality, and like the park itself, both the **Naval Museum** (open daily 9am–5pm; admission fee) with naval hardware at the far western end of the park and the **Aquarium and Black Sea Museum** (open Tues–Sun 9am–5pm; admission fee) have seen better days, but both remain favourites with children. Also popular with children are the **Planetarium** (shows every 90 minutes 9am–3.30pm; admission fee) and the **Dolphinarium** (shows every two hours from 10am; admission fee) at the other end of the park. The **Natural History Museum** (open daily 9.30am–6pm; admission fee) is far better, featuring a large number of live spiders, snakes, crabs, frogs, geckos and rodents in the small zoo in a side building of the museum.

Soviet coastguard vessel in Primorski Park's Naval Museum

Golden Sands

Known to Bulgarians as Zlatni Pyusatsi, **Golden Sands** (Златни Пясъци) is a sprawling, purpose-built seaside resort 18km (11 miles) north of Varna. A staple of Western European holiday brochures, it is the best known of all the Bulgarian beach resorts. A package holiday is still the best way of visiting the resort, as hotel rack rates are far higher than those offered by travel agencies and tour operators.

Although perhaps not quite golden, the 5km (3-mile) beach is fabulous, sloping gently to the sea, and offering every water sport from parascending and water-skiing to jet-skiing and windsurfing at various points along its length. The resort's small marina is at the northern end of the resort, beyond which is a nudist beach. There is a water park, **Aquapolis**, behind the resort on the other side of the main road from Varna to Balchik.

Golden girls at Golden Sands

There are more than 70 hotels of all categories in the resort, all now in private hands and fully refurbished. Not all of the resort's hotels are on the seafront, however, and some are quite a way from the beach. Though there is no real centre to this artificial resort, there is a collection of shops and banks around the **Church of St John**.

Most package holiday-makers eat in their hotels, though there are plenty of restaurants throughout the resort, and an endless number of bars and discos. The International Hotel has a casino. The resort is linked to Varna by numerous taxis (make sure you take a taxi displaying the name and phone number of a taxi company) and by bus No. 9 from the southern end of the resort to Varna cathedral. The journey takes about 20 minutes.

Aladzha Monastery

In a forest northwest of Golden Sands are the remains of the rock-hewn Aladzha Monastery (open Tues–Sun 10am–5pm; admission fee), founded in the 14th century and populated by the Hesychast order of monks until the 18th century. There is a small museum that shows how the monastery looked when it was occupied.

Albena

Currently the trendiest and consequently most expensive of the Black Sea resorts, **Albena** (Албена), 30km (18 miles) from Varna, is smaller than Golden Sands and a lot younger; until 1970 there wasn't a hotel in sight. Today the step-pyramid conceptual creations come as something of a pleasant surprise after the straight lines of Golden Sands. The resort is increasingly popular with Bulgaria's smart set and less frequented by package tourists.

The beach itself is wider, whiter and quieter than Golden Sands, though there is less scope for water sports. There is an excellent **equestrian centre** next to the Malibu Hotel, which offers riding lessons and horse-back excursions into the surrounding countryside.

Balchik

The fact that the small town of **Balchik** (Балчик), 15km (10 miles) north of Albena, was made famous by Romania's Queen Marie, Queen Victoria's granddaughter, who had her summer residence here, highlights the difficult history of the

Dobruja region. Lost to Romania after the Balkan Wars, Balchik and the rest of the Dobruja was only returned to Bulgaria by Hitler in 1940. Since then it has become a resort popular with elderly Bulgarians, who find the place a quiet retreat. The lack of a beach deters the majority of tourists.

That does not stop the package tourists, though, who come here for day-trips to the **Tenha Yuva** complex (the palace of Queen Marie, open 8am–5pm; admission fee) throughout the summer. The simple palace itself, set on a hilltop overlooking the town, is dominated by a minaret-like tower and betrays Marie, who insisted on designing almost every detail herself, as a rather unsophisticated architect. A number of other buildings are far lovelier, including a stone summer house from where Marie watched the sea. The complex's botanical garden is home to more than 3,000 rare and exotic plants. Some 4km (2 miles) from Balchik is **Tuzlata**, a tiny resort famous for its mud treatments.

Bourgas and Surroundings

The largest town on the southern part of the coast, the important port and industrial city of **Bourgas** (Бурғас), has little to offer the visitor and, with the far more attractive towns of Pomorie, Nessebur and Sozopol all close by, it should be used only as a stopping-off point or day-trip destination at best.

Pomorie (Поморие), around 20km (13 miles) northeast of Bourgas, is situated on a slim, rocky peninsula separating the bay of Bourgas from the Black Sea, and has been offering mud treatments for well over 2,000 years. All of the town's hotels double as mud treatment centres, and it is difficult to find a room unless you are booked into one of the clinics. Besides mud, the town is known for salt – and wine; local Pamid, Dimyat and Merlots are among the country's best. Though narrow and often very crowded, the village's beach is excellent.

Nessebur

A further 18km (11 miles) further north is **Nessebur** (Несебър), which has Bulgaria's best beach and some of its best preserved 19th-century wooden architecture. Split in two by a slim causeway, Nessebur is famous mainly for its old town, situated on the peninsula that juts awkwardly into the Black Sea. The town's narrow, cobbled streets, wooden houses and medieval churches are as much an emblem of Bulgaria as Dubrovnik is of Croatia.

Entering Old Nessebur via its **Town Gate**, with **fortifications** dating back to the 6th century on either side, it is possible to imagine how impregnable the town must have been. Once inside, the **Archaeological Museum** (on the right as you enter, open Mar–Oct daily 9am–7pm; admission fee) is a good introduction to the town's history. From there, magnificent **churches** await exploration; there were once more than 40 on the peninsula and many remain worthy of your time today. Following a roughly clockwise route around the peninsula, the first one that you will see is the 14th-century **Church of the Holy Pantocrator**, whose exterior marks it out as one of the finest medieval churches in the country. Next is the **Church of St John the Baptist**, an 11th-century church

Nessebur, highlight of the coast

Best for seafood

Nessebur, at the centre of the Bulgarian Black Sea's fishing industry, is the best place on the coast to enjoy seafood.

somewhat caught between the simple designs of the early Christians and the more complex, ornate churches that followed. Following ul Alehoi, the next church you encounter is the 14th-century **Church of Archangels Michael and Gabriel**, a stunning example of medieval craftsmanship, while next to that is the less impressive **Church of Sv Paraskeva** of the same era. Further on is the **Church of Sv Bogodoritsa**, while on the seashore are the ruins of the **Basilica**, which date from the 5th century.

Inland, in the middle of the endlessly busy central square, **pl Mitropolitska**, the 5th-century **Old Bishopric (Sv Sofia)** stands in ruins, while its counterpart, the **New Bishopric (Sv Stefan)** on ul Rilbarska, is a much-rebuilt church dating from the 11th century. The frescoes date from the 17th century, while the pulpit and bishop's throne were added in the 18th century. The 14th-century **Church of St John Aliturgitus** at the end of the same street is the best of Nessebur's churches. Perched high above the harbour, its bizarre exterior tops anything else in the town.

Sunny Beach

Just north of Nessebur is the enormous beach resort of **Sunny Beach**, Slanchev Bryag (Сльнчав Вряг) in Bulgarian. More than 100 hotels stretch along the narrow 7km (4-mile) beach, and while investment continues, with almost all of the hotels refurbished and now in private hands, the resort is still a little shabby, and the least satisfactory of all the coast resorts. That said, it is cheap, offers great opportunities for water sports, and has some of the best hotels on the coast. There are also more than 50 restaurants and terraces, and an endless number of bars and discos.

Sozopol

Approximately 30km (21 miles) south of Bourgas, **Sozopol** (Созопол), just about the last town on the coast, could well be the best. An ancient fishing village on a peninsula much like Nessebur, Sozopol's distance from a large package holiday resort means that it does not get the day-trippers that crowd Nessebur, making it a far better place to wander around.

Like Nessebur, Sozopol is divided into old and new parts, Old Sozopol, on the peninsula, being the most popular destination for visitors. The causeway that links the two parts acts as the town's unofficial centre, and it is always awash with hawkers selling less-than-impressive souvenirs. The rather ordinary **Archaeological Museum** (open Mon–Fri 10am–5pm; admission fee) stands on the south of the causeway. To the right is a small park containing two of Sozopol's Revival-period churches, the **Church of Sv Zosim** and the **Church of Sts Cyril and Methodius**, below which is the private Raiski Beach (admission fee). **Old Sozopol** is a warren of narrow cobbled streets, wooden houses, churches, cafés, restaurants and souvenir shops.

Every September Sozopol hosts the Apollonia Arts Festival, with opera, classical music and theatre, during which the town is swamped with visitors.

Wooden houses in Sozopol

WHAT TO DO

SPORTS AND OUTDOOR PURSUITS

Skiing

Bulgaria has been a popular destination for budget-conscious skiers for a number of years. The three main resorts of Borovets, Pamporovo and Vitosha, which are stalwarts in package-tour brochures, have recently been joined by a fourth, Bansko, now one of the most modern ski resorts in Europe.

There is usually good snow cover in all of the resorts from late December to the end of March, and you can also ski on the highest slopes at Vitosha and Bansko well into April. While the skiing is good, however, it is not particularly extensive or challenging. As a rule of thumb, Pamporovo is best suited to beginners, Borovets and Bansko for intermediate skiers, while Vitosha offers the most difficult slopes in the country.

Vitosha apart, all the resorts are well appointed with a variety of hotels and places to hire ski equipment. You will pay far more if arriving on spec than if you book accommodation and ski hire before departure. Lift pass prices are increasing, although they are still low by Western-European standards – around 30 leva per day. Note that at Borovets and Vitosha one or two lifts are privately operated and are not covered by the lift pass. Ask which lifts are covered when buying your pass.

All of Bulgaria's ski resorts are crowded at the weekend, when city-dwellers swarm all over them. Vitosha, just 15km (10 miles) from Sofia, is the worst affected, so expect long queues and crowded pistes on Saturday and Sunday. During the week, however, you may well have the slopes to yourself.

Vitosha offers some of Bulgaria's toughest ski slopes

Hiking and Walking

As spring gives way to summer, skiers give way to hikers and walkers, both locals and international tourists. Unpredictable weather in late spring can mean that snow and freezing temperatures grip the mountains as late as the end of May. The season begins in earnest in June.

Hiking is one of the most popular activities in the country, so hikers are well catered for. The best areas are the Pirin, Rila and Rhodope mountains, all three ranges offering a large number of well marked routes. For longer hikes you will need to be in possession of a good map before setting off. These can be bought in all good bookshops in Sofia, or in hotels in mountain resorts. Always check weather conditions before heading off; even in high summer the weather can turn in an instant at high altitude.

In Bulgarian hiking country

Most routes are dotted with small cabins – usually open only during summer – where you can buy refreshments and, sometimes, spend the night for just a few leva.

Mountain Biking

Mountain biking is a relatively new pursuit in Bulgaria, as indeed is biking of any sort. There are a number of marked tracks laid out especially for mountain bikers, the best at Pamporovo and Bansko. Unless you are bringing your own bike, head for a ski resort, where you will be able to rent a bike in good condition from a large hotel, such as the Rila or Samokov in Borovets, the Pamporovo and Finlandia in Pamporovo, or the Pirin and Bansko in Bansko.

Golf

Bulgaria has gone golf mad, with three 18-hole courses opening in recent times. The

Sailing in Nessebur Harbour

closest to the capital is the 5,335-m (5,836-yds) par-71 course at the Air Sofia Leisure Club, which is about 50km (30 miles) from Sofia in the village of Ihtiman, halfway along the Sofia–Plovdiv highway. There is another par-71 course at Sliven, and a par-70 course close to the north-eastern town of Razgrad.

Golf is not cheap and the green fees are high. The three courses charge around 70 leva per round, although prices are cheaper off season and early in the morning. For more details visit <www.golf-bg.com>.

Sailing

Increasingly popular among the nouveaux riches, leisure sailing centres on Golden Sands, the plushest of the Black Sea resorts, and there are 11 marinas up and down the coast. The most popular are the Golden Sands Marina, Port Varna Marina Club and the Bourgas Yacht Club. All three have boats for hire, though you will need proof of your sailing credentials.

Football

Bulgarians are mad about football, which remains the most popular spectator sport by some way. The country's finest

Levski football stadium in Sofia

hour came in 1994 when the national team – led by the legendary Hristo Stoichkov – narrowly lost to Italy in the World Cup semi-final, and while the current side is bereft of the big names of the 1994 side, it did manage to qualify for the 2004 European Championship, where it performed badly. After an unsuccessful qualifying campaign for Germany 2006, Stoichkov took over as national team coach. He lasted less than a year.

Although most stars now ply their trade abroad at wealthier clubs, domestic football is still hotly contested, and matches between the most popular teams (Levski and CSKA Sofia, Litex Lovech, Lokomotiv Plovdiv) attract large crowds. The season runs from July to June, with a break from December to March.

Hunting

Bulgaria's varied countryside presents opportunities to hunt big and small game, including deer, wild boar, bears, pheasants, ducks and partridges. The rules governing the sport are strict, with annual quotas for each species. Payment is determined by species and size. Shooting a pheasant may cost just a few leva, while hunting a large brown bear may cost thousands of euros. Hunters need an international hunting licence and must have special permits to bring their guns into the country.

If you want to hunt in Bulgaria, it is best to have a local travel agent take care of all the paperwork. A number of travel agents specialise in hunting holidays, including Sofia-based EuroHunters <www.eurohunters.com> and Stara Zagora-based Stival <www.bulgaria.com/hunting>.

Fishing

Fishing is popular all over the country. Fresh-water fishing is especially good in the Rila Mountains where, depending on the season, you can find carp, mullet, pike and pike-perch, with only May (the spawning season) off-limits. The Black Sea offers huge numbers of salt-water fish, including turbot, mackerel and tunny fish. There is no angling off-season on the coast. A small dog shark is also found in the Black Sea and it can be fished from a boat around 4km (2 miles) off the coast. Most Sofia tour agencies can make arrangements for angling safaris.

Birdwatching

Once a well-kept secret, Bulgaria's reputation for birdwatching has become more widely known in recent years, and the country is fast becoming one of Europe's top birdwatching destinations. Two areas in particular offer a great range of bird species: the marshlands around Bourgas and the Madzharovo nature reserve in the Rhodope Mountains. The more than 500 kinds of bird that either nest in Bulgaria in spring or pass through on migration in the autumn, include the Dalmatian pelican, glossy ibis, spoonbill, black stork, pygmy

Stork on a stopover

cormorant, ferruginous duck, Egyptian, black and griffon vultures, Levant sparrowhawk, long-legged buzzard, peregrine falcon and white-tailed, golden and eastern imperial eagles.

Among the tour operators offering birdwatching excursions is Sofia-based Pandion <www.birdwatchingholidays.com>, which can help with all aspects of birdwatching, from booking hotels to tailor-made, fully escorted tours. Pandion also offers butterfly- and dragonfly-spotting tours. Independent birdwatchers should come in spring to Pamporovo, a good base in the Rhodopes, and to Bourgas in the autumn. Even the casual observer will, however, notice a profusion of birdlife at any time of year in almost any rural setting.

SHOPPING

Bulgaria is by no means a shopper's paradise, but it does offer some of the best shopping in the Balkans. During the Communist period there wasn't much to interest anyone, and while Bulgarian shops were never as barren and depressingly deserted as their Romanian counterparts, it was still difficult to purchase many consumer goods without having to wait for some time. All that has changed. Economic reform may not have been as fast as that of other former Communist countries, but when it comes to consumer commerce, the Bulgarians now lead the way.

In the days of the 'wild East' – immediately following the collapse of the Communist regime – almost anything could be bought for any price. Although those days have gone, you will still find a few forbidden fruits in the country's flea markets, most notably counterfeit CDs and DVDs, production of which is one of the country's biggest industries (see page 90).

Shops in general are open all day until around 6pm. Note that customer service is still non-existent. Credit cards are now accepted in all but the smallest stores, although using one invariably provokes muttering.

Markets and Malls

Prices in general can be divided into two categories: cheap (if the product is made in Bulgaria) and expensive (if the product is imported). While haggling has long been a Balkan necessity, it is now frowned upon in all but the most provincial markets. Try it in a chic boutique in Sofia and the police may be called.

Most of Bulgaria's groceries are still purchased early in the morning at markets, and produce is strictly seasonal. Imported goods can be found out of season only in expensive supermarkets. Almost everything else is sold in standard high-street shops or malls. The biggest mall is City Center Sofia: 44,000 sq m (474,000 sq ft) of retail therapy. There are also a number of flea markets for those who know where to look. The biggest and best is the one in front of the Alexander Nevski Cathedral in Sofia. If you are looking for a genuine Third Reich fountain pen, then this is the place to

Produce at the Zhenski Pasar (Women's Market) in Sofia

Gourds in Melnik

come, while busts of Lenin and Stalin and posters of Todor Zhivkov and other Communist heroes are also popular. Russian army hats are two a penny, while medals, watches and other Soviet memorabilia – all of which may or may not be original – can be bought for peanuts. Directly next to the flea market is another one, selling Orthodox iconography and naive art which, while not cheap, is good quality and a very good place to hunt for souvenirs.

The Black Sea coast's numerous street hawkers sell little else but sunglasses, beachwear and accessories, most of which is terribly poor in terms of quality. Ski resorts attract the winter equivalent of these hawkers. Sports shops in the ski resorts can offer bargain ski equipment, as a number of Western brands manufacture in Bulgaria under licence, and prices for skis and ski boots are much cheaper here than in Western Europe, especially after the end of February.

What to Buy

Traditional Bulgarian handicrafts offer a wide choice of wares. These include lace, pottery, woodcarvings and iconography. Bulgarian souvenir shops are ubiquitous, though the souvenirs themselves can be of variable quality.

Reproductions of **Orthodox iconography** and **wood carvings** can be bought all over the country, with the best quality being found in Sofia in the art market outside the Alexander Nevski Cathedral. As a general rule, the stuff sold by hawkers and stallholders outside the more famous

Bulgarian monasteries should be bought only in a souvenir emergency, as quality is patchy at best.

If you are after **genuine antique icons**, as opposed to re-productions, you should contact a professional art dealer and have a reasonable idea of what you are looking for. Exporting antiques is a difficult process requiring a long paper chase that a dealer will be able to handle with ease. Only the brave should attempt to do it on their own. There are a number of galleries in Sofia clustered together on the streets around the Radisson Hotel. Any of them will be delighted to help.

The manufacture of **fine pottery** in this part of the world dates back as far as the Thracians, and the work of Bulgarian potters is traditionally sacred, with know-how a closely guarded secret kept within families of potters. Pottery re-ally first flourished during the 12th to 14th centuries, only to go into abeyance during the Turkish Yoke, before being resurrected during the National Revival period. This is when Berkovitsa and Gab-rovo became bywords for ex-cellence in the field, their green, brown and yellow cre-ations a Bulgarian trade-mark. Over the last hundred years or so the craft has somewhat died out, and today only a few potteries re-main, mostly as working mu-seums. The **Etura complex** near Gabrovo *(see page 66)* is

Icons in Varna

a fine example of this kind of living museum and an excellent place to purchase exquisite handmade Bulgarian pottery, as is the market in pl Samodivska in **Veliko Tarnovo**.

Etura is also a good location to find **embroidery and lace**, though the best place is probably along the coast, especially in Varna, as there is so much choice and competition between the old ladies who throng the market that surrounds the Cathedral of the Virgin Mary. Quality here is high and prices are reasonable, though not cheap. You can try haggling but few of these *babushki* speak any English, and may not understand your attempts to get the price of an item down.

Where to Shop

Sofia. Vitosha Boulevard is the country's top shopping street, though you will not find anything here that cannot be bought (often cheaper) in your home country. The best souvenir shops in the capital are those on the second floor of the TZUM department store and in the underpass leading from the Presidency to the Largo. The Halite grocery market can be fun in the early mornings, while the Zhenski Pazar (Women's Market) is another good place to hunt for bargains. Graf

Faking It

Bulgaria remains one of the world's largest producers of fake CDs and DVDs, despite repeated calls from the European Union to stamp out their production, retail and export. The government makes occasional high-profile raids on illegal factories, but these do little real damage to what is a multi-billion euro industry. All Bulgarian towns and cities are full of street retailers brazenly offering discs for sale, usually a mind-boggling selection of the most up-to-date music, as well as back-catalogues. In most cases if the vendor does not have the particular album you are looking for, he will have one made for you overnight.

Ignatiev Boulevard is home to an excellent second-hand book market, as well as an outlet for counterfeit CDs and DVDs. There are now also two big modern malls in Sofia: the Mall of Sofia, on the city's outskirts, and City Center Sofia, closer to the centre of town.

Plovdiv. The pedestrian only Alexander I Boulevard, which leads from pl Tsentralen towards Old Plovdiv, is the city's foremost shopping throughfare, and has numerous cafés, restaurants and bars. There is an excellent daily market situated on ul Raichio, on the southern side of pl Tsentralen, where good, cheap forgeries of all your favourite brand-name clothes are a speciality.

Shopping in Plovdiv centres around Alexander I Boulevard

Varna. Knyaz Boris I Boulevard, from pl Nezavisimost to Tsar Osvoboditel Boulevard, has perhaps the best selection of shops anywhere in Bulgaria. All the major international brand names have boutiques on the street, and these often sit side by side with discount stores selling counterfeit versions of the same goods. Varna is also home to a number of nautical shops, some selling tacky souvenirs, others selling professional sailing gear. The market outside the cathedral is the best place in the country to find lace and embroidery, although the flea market situated on the other side of the main road sells only rubbish to tourists who should know better.

ENTERTAINMENT

Nightlife and Café Culture

Before 1990 the only nightlife on offer in the entire country comprised tacky hotel discos, cabarets on the Black Sea and the casino at the Sheraton. Private enterprise has changed all that, with clubs, discos, Irish pubs and cafés opening everywhere. Note, however, that if sophistication and state-of-the-art technology are your thing, you will be disappointed.

Given its sheer size and wide choice of bars and discos, Sofia is probably best for nightlife, while all of the Black Sea resorts, especially Golden Sands and Sunny Beach, have a reputation for long, long nights and also have a number of casinos. Varna, too, has a profusion of good discos along its seafront. The ski resorts, catering mainly for foreign tourists, also have good night-time options, while the student town of Blagoevgrad is a major nightlife centre for the young during term-time.

Cultural Performances

The cultural capital of the country remains Plovdiv, where the Roman Amphitheatre stages world-class music and theatre throughout the summer. Varna also has a number of festivals, including the Varna International Pop Music Festival, held at various venues throughout the city every May, with performers of variable ability, though there is usually at least one major international star. Far more satisfactory is the Varna Classical Summer Festival, held every June and featuring big names from the world of Bulgarian and international music and opera.

The Sofia National Opera is the country's most famous opera, though the standard of performances depends on the singers on stage on any particular night, as those most in demand are often performing elsewhere.

The National Theatre stages Bulgarian and international drama

There are good operas at Blagoevgrad, Varna and Plovdiv. The country's best performers congregate at Plovdiv in the summer when they perform at the amphitheatre. Tickets are invariably cheap and represent excellent value for money.

Folk Music

Among connoisseurs, traditional Bulgarian music – especially female singing – is respected and renowned worldwide. It may well be one day enjoyed in other galaxies – one of the *Voyager* rockets launched in the 1970s, in the hope of it eventually being picked up by other life forms, includes a Bulgarian folk song from the Rhodopes on a gilded copper gramophone record.

To hear Bulgarian music closer to earth, you should head for the Pirin Song Festival held every August, or buy any of the excellent compilation cassettes and CDs of Bulgarian music that can be found in music stores and souvenir shops.

A bagpiper at the festival in Mugla *(see page 96)*

Traditional instruments include the *gaida* (bagpipes), the *kaval* (shepherd's pipes), the *brumbuzuk* (a small pipe) and *chans* (sheep's bells). All are impossibly difficult to play but make extraordinary music when performed well. One of the best places to see traditional music being performed is at any restaurant offering a folk programme. Though often designed for tourists, they are usually very good value.

Kukeri Festivals

Almost certainly Thracian in origin, the Kukeri festivals are probably the most bewildering sights in Bulgaria for the uninitiated. At various times throughout the year – usually at New Year or in spring – participants (always male) dress up in animal skins – including elaborate, fearsome masks often made from animal heads – and enter a trance-like state before parading through towns and villages manically chanting, dancing, shouting, singing, and generally acting in a way that will make evil spirits think twice before returning. The parades can last all day and mock executions are often enacted to symbolise the death of winter.

As recently as the 19th century, the tradition was common all over the country but today just a few large Kukeri festivals remain. The best places to see them are: Pernik, a small town 25km (15 miles) west of Sofia, during the last weekend of January; and Shiroka Luka, close to Pamporovo, on the first Sunday in March.

CHILDREN'S BULGARIA

Bulgaria's seaside and ski resorts are terrific destinations for families, as accommodation is excellent value and children's activities are relatively cheap. There are water parks up and down the Black Sea coast, with plenty of places to swim or try water sports. Do be careful when taking part in any water sports, however, as not all sports centres have the correct authorisation. Best head for an activity centre attached to a good hotel. Shows at the dolphinarium in Varna are popular with children of all ages.

Three of the main ski resorts – Bansko, Borovets and Pamporovo – have specialist children's ski schools that organise snow crèches, children's races and other competitions. Bansko is the favourite resort of families as it offers other, non-skiing activities such as ice skating and sleigh rides.

There are many things for children to do in and around Sofia, from ceramic painting on the ground floor of TZUM to Sofia Zoo, which has large, open areas for children to explore in safety. The Sofia Land amusement park is more than enough to keep children happy for an afternoon. The Puppet Theatre in Sofia, at 14 ul Gurko, will also keep children amused, even though all performances are in Bulgarian. There is a children's swimming pool at the Hotel Princess, and all the major hotels organise Sunday brunches with entertainment for children.

Bulgarians in general love children and will go out of their way to accommodate them. The main problem with children is keeping them amused while travelling from place to place, as roads are poor and trains slow, meaning that travelling times can be long.

Food should not be a problem, as Bulgarians themselves are not fond of spicy foods, while universal children's favourites, such as omelettes, or steak with chips, are found on every menu in the country.

Calendar of Festivals

Many festivals in Bulgaria follow the old, Julian calendar, in which Easter usually falls a week or two after the Western Easter.

January/February New Year's Day, known as St Vassal's (St Basil's) Day, is celebrated in the Pernik and Dupnitsa regions with Kukeri festivals. Some parts of the country still celeberate Christmas Day according to the old calendar, on 6 January.

March Kukeri festival at Shiroka Luka, first Sunday in March.

April Orthodox Easter is best celebrated at the Alexander Nevski Cathedral in Sofia or at Rila Monastery.

May Varna International Pop Festival takes place during the last week of May; the International Biennale of Humour and Satire is held in Gabrovo in odd-numbered years. The Koprovshtitsa Folklore Festival straddles May and June.

June The Festival of the Roses takes place in Kazanlak during the first weekend of June; Varna International Music and Theatre Festival is held every year towards the end of the month.

July Verdi Festival held in Plovdiv during the first week of July.

August Folk festivals in Bourgas and Varna; the Festival of the Sea in Balchik and Sozopol; the Dunov Festival in the Rila lakes; the Pirin Song Festival: dates are not fixed. The Rozhen Sings festival takes place during the last week of August; the Bagpipe Festival at Mugla is held on the last Sunday of August. Assumption Day (15 August) is celebrated with ritual processions at any church that has a temporal connection with the Virgin Mary.

September The Krustova Gora Festival of the Cross takes place on 14 September, celebrated in Bulgaria as Day of the Cross; the Apollonia Arts Festival in Sozopol, with performances of opera, classical music and theatre, held on the causeway.

October St John of Rila day at Rila Monastery; wine harvest festival in Melnik (both on 18 October).

December Kukeri festivals on Christmas Day in Blagoevgrad.

EATING OUT

Bulgaria's cuisine is unquestionably tasty, but it can be very heavy, and the ingredients used are not always of the highest standard. All meats except pork – which is always exceptional – can be patchy in quality and have to be cooked well. Unfortunately, local know-how suffered during the Communist period and, though culinary discipline is improving as more international restaurants open, bringing international chefs and their skills, improvement is slow. This does not mean that you will have any trouble eating well in Bulgaria; it simply means that to find high-class, international-standard meals you should stick to the best hotels and restaurants of Sofia and the larger towns and cities. In the country's smaller towns and cities you will have to go local, though doing so can sometimes be rewarding.

Café society in Sofia

Voluntarily going without meat is still a strange concept to most people in Bulgaria, and vegetarians will struggle, despite the fact that a great variety of tasty vegetarian dishes, such as *chuski biurek* – peppers stuffed with beans and cheese – are cooked as a matter of course day in, day out in any number of home kitchens. The problem is finding such dishes on a restaurant menu. You won't.

Light breakfasts of coffee with bread and yoghurt are followed by an early lunch of considerable proportions. Evening meals are taken late, around 9pm or even later. The main Easter meal is eaten after midnight mass on Saturday night. Such meals, especially in large families, can often go on all night.

Local Ingredients

The quality of pork *(svinsko)* is of the highest order throughout the Balkans, and Bulgaria is no exception. One of the main staples, it appears in any number of dishes. Chicken and veal are also popular and most other meats are readily available. Beef tends to be expensive and not always of the best quality.

Local ingredients from the Women's Market in Sofia

Though Bulgaria has a not insignificant coastline, fish is not as available as it should be, even on the coast. Carp, trout and perch are the most common local fish, and are usually grilled and served plain with boiled potatoes. Nessebur has the coast's best selection of seafood restaurants. All along the coast you will find street vendors selling *tsatsi*, small, sardine-like fish fried in a rudimentary batter and covered in salt. They taste great.

Given the fact that Bulgarians claim to have invented yoghurt, known locally as *kiselo mlyako*, they make no bones about adding it to almost any dish. If you are unsure about whether your food will come smothered in yoghurt, ask: *Mozhe li da prigotvite yastieto bes kiselo mlyako?* Can you make this dish without yoghurt?

Mouthwatering melons are available in late summer

Bulgarian fruit and vegetables are of excellent quality, though strictly seasonal. Agriculture is slowly adopting Western techniques and practices, but most produce remains organic, and as a result tastes superb. Tomatoes especially have a flavour that long ago disappeared from the supermarkets of Western countries. Sweetcorn is popular in season (August and early September) and you will find street vendors selling boiled cobs all over the country. Melons, both water and honeydew, are fabulous and appear at the end of July. Prices are high at the beginning of the season, but by the end of September they are all but given away.

Bulgarian bread, which accompanies every dish, is usually dusted with oil and served hot.

Popular Dishes

Defining what is actually Bulgarian national cuisine, as opposed to what is merely Balkan, is difficult. Dishes that the Bulgarians claim as their own, such as *shkembe chorba* (tripe soup) or *kashkaval pane* (fried, breaded cheese) for instance, are just as likely to be found in Macedonia,

Yoghurt salad served in a *mehana*

Romania, Serbia and even Turkey. There are, of course, local variations that go beyond differences in spelling, and pure Bulgarian dishes include *sirene po shopski* (baked goat's cheese) and *kavarma* (meat and vegetable stew, often very spicy). Other popular dishes include *tarator* (a thick cold yoghurt and cucumber soup, often served as a starter), *kiopolou* (roasted or grilled aubergines and peppers, often served covered in vinegar), *kiuftete* (meat balls, either pork or chicken, usually flattened out to look like hamburger patties), *chuski biurek* (fried or baked peppers stuffed with beans and cheese) and *giuvech* (a thick stew usually served in the pot it was cooked in, and a staple of all Bulgarian-cuisine restaurants).

When it comes to snacks, Bulgarians love savouries: you will see *gevrek* (a kind of bagel topped with salt) and *banit-sa* (a light pastry filled with cheese) sold everywhere; they are best eaten piping hot. *Semki* (sunflower seeds) are eaten as though they were the last food in the world. Go to a football match in Bulgaria and by the end of the game you will be knee-deep in sunflower seed shells.

You will find that Bulgarian desserts tend to consist of very sweet Turkish derivatives, such as *baklava* or *revane*. *Halvitsa*, a kind of nougat, is also popular, but it is rarely found in restaurants. Ice-cream sellers litter the country's streets all summer long.

Where to Eat

There are now a large number of Bulgarian restaurants, known as *mehana*, where traditional dishes are served, often accompanied by a folklore show of variable taste and quality. Choice is usually limited in these establishments, however, and you may often hear the phrase *Za sezhalenie ... svershi* (We do not have...).

Yoghurt

Bulgarians invented yoghurt, or so they will tell you. Certainly, people in the region have made yoghurt throughout history to preserve milk, much in the same way as Northern Europeans have made cheese and butter. The earliest yoghurts were probably spontaneously fermented, perhaps by wild bacteria residing inside goatskin bags used for transport. It was originally produced exclusively on a domestic scale, using sheep's milk. The word for yoghurt comes from the Turkish verb *yogurtmak* (to blend), but its active ingredient is called *Lactobacillus bulgaricus*, a fact that only supports the Bulgarian claim to have invented it.

Yoghurt remains today a staple of the Bulgarian diet. It is often taken at breakfast, though it can be drunk at any time throughout the day. It is also used as an ingredient in many Bulgarian dishes, the most popular of which is the cold soup *tarator*.

The *mehana* is the place for traditional Bulgarian food

Though you should try Bulgaria's main dishes, at some stage you may want something a little more familiar. The Black Sea coast is full of dubious establishments with such names as London Pub or Wembley Pride, all serving the standard English fried breakfast and roast beef lunches. Sofia has some fine international restaurants, including the now legendary Japanese restaurant at the Kempinski Hotel. Chinese food is also popular among Bulgarians and you will find Chinese restaurants all over the country, even in the most remote of towns. Finding a good Indian meal is impossible outside of Sofia.

Side dishes

When eating out, especially in traditional Bulgarian restaurants, make sure you ask the waiter if the dish you have ordered will be accompanied by a *garnitura* (side dish). It is usual in this country to order and pay for everything separately, including bread.

What to Drink
Wine

Grape cultivation and wine producing in Bulgaria dates back to antiquity. The Pomorie region has been known for wine since the Thracians planted the first vines around 1500BC. Today wine is grown in most parts of the country and exported to Europe, the US, Japan and China. The state-owned vineyards have nearly all been privatised, and quality has rocketed, though to give the devil his due, the Communist state's monopoly Vinprom was investing heavily in Australian and American machinery and know-how in the 1970s and 1980s, which laid the foundation for the excellent wines produced today.

There are five main wine regions: Eastern, Northern, Sub-Balkan, Southern and South-Western. The best white wine tends to come from the Eastern region, as the warmth and moisture of the coastal air add fruitiness to the grapes. The leading labels of the region are Jambol and Stambolovo.

Red wines are the speciality of the Northern region and the vineyards around Ruse on the Danubian plain. Use of the noble Cabernet Sauvignon, which is especially suited to the cooler, damper soil and long warm autumns, is common, though local varieties of grape are also used. The leading wineries are those at Ruse, Suhindol and Ljaskovets.

The other regions are less noted, with a couple of exceptions. The Sungulare Misket and Sungulare Eau de Vie are whites of abundant flavour from the depths of the Balkan valleys, while perhaps the most famous Bulgarian wine, the fruity white Misket of the Valley of the Roses, is produced in the Sub-Balkan region. The most famous winery in the country is that in Assenovgrad, which produces the Mavrud and Gamza reds.

You will find a good selection of wines at all supermarkets throughout the country, though there are also a number of specialist wine merchants in Sofia, Plovdiv, Rousse, Varna and Bourgas. Purchasing wine direct from a winery tends not to be any cheaper than doing so from ordinary shops, and you are likely to be limited to the wines bottled at the vineyard.

Spirits

The local spirit is *rakia*, made of prunes or grapes, often at home. You can buy *rakia* in supermarkets, but the home-brewed stuff is best. It is often drunk as an aperitif, and if you are invited to a Bulgarian home you will simply not be able to escape trying it. Do not resist; embrace its charm. The taste is something that can be acquired afterwards. Another popular local drink is *boza*, a thick, slightly alcoholic and rather sickly brown juice made from wheat, barley or corn.

Selection of wines and spirits from the Pomorie region

Beer

This is produced in abundance and is much more popular with locals than wine. Most breweries are owned by major international companies and quality is always high. The leading local brands are Boliarka from Veliko Tarnovo, Astika from Haskovo and Gold from the Zagorka brewery in Stara Zagora. Boliarka also produces a bizarre stout called Stolichno. Beer is almost always bought in bottles, even in pubs, and pubs selling draught beers are rare, even in Sofia. Imported beers are widely available but expensive.

Wate...
Bulgarian t... to drink, but... ber of springs... throughout the... makes bottled w... cheap that almost ...re population eschews ...he tap.

901

To Help You Order...

Can I see the menu?	**Izvinete munyuto, molya?**
I'm a vegetarian.	**Az sum vegetarianets.**
Can I have a beer, please?	**Edna bira, molya.**
Please may I have the bill.	**Smetkata, molya.**

beef	**govezhdo**	meatball	**kiufte**
beer	**bira**	milk	**mlyako**
boiled	**vereni**	mineral	**mineralna**
potatoes	**kartofi**	water	**voda**
bread	**khlyap**	omelette	**omlet**
carp	**sharan**	pepper	**piper**
cheese	**sirene**	pork	**svinsko**
chicken	**pileshko**	rice	**oris**
chips	**perzheni**	salad	**salata**
(French fries)	**kartofi**	salmon	**syomga**
coffee	**kafe**	salt	**sol**
fish	**riba**	sausages	**karnache**
honey	**met**	schnitzel	**shnitzel**
juice	**sok**	scrambled	**barkani**
kebab	**kebap**	eggs	**yaitsa**
lamb	**agneshko**	steak	**biftek**
mackerel	**skumriya**	tea	**chay**
mashed	**kartofeno**	trout	**pestarva**
potatoes	**piuray**	wine	**vino**

HANDY TRAVEL TIPS

An A–Z Summary of Practical Information

A

ACCOMMODATION

Almost every town, city and resort has a wide choice of accommodation. The Black Sea coast and ski resorts offer the widest range, though Sofia, which has a number of five-star establishments, is catching up fast. In other cities you will sometimes be hard pushed to find top-class hotels, but there is always somewhere comfortable and fairly luxurious on offer. Even the lowliest bed-and-breakfast will offer satellite or cable television, and internet access is also standard.

Note that hotels on the Black Sea and in ski resorts are much cheaper if booked via an agency, either in Bulgaria or abroad and, during peak beach and ski season, will insist on a minimum stay, usually three nights. Ask if there are any deals; in Sofia, even five-star hotel rates can be negotiated, especially at the weekend

I'd like a...	**Bi iskal...**
single room	**edinichna staya**
double room	**dvoina staya**
with a bath	**sbanya**
with a shower	**sdush**
What's the rate per day?	**Kolko struva stayata?**
I have a reservation.	**Rezerviral sem staya.**
Do you have any vacancies?	**Imate li svobodna staya?**

AIRPORTS

Sofia, Plovdiv, Varna and Bourgas have international airports. Airports at Ruse and Gorna Orjahovica have irregular services to and from Sofia, and Varna in the summer.

Sofia's airport – the country's largest and busiest – has had a facelift and is now a modern, efficient facility. Baggage usually arrives promptly and the only queues – which can be long at peak times – are at passport control. A host of yellow, metered taxis wait outside and should cover the 15-km (10-mile) journey to the centre of town for around 20 leva. Make sure the taxi displays the name 'OK Supertrans' on its doors.

Plovdiv, used primarily by ski charters in winter, is even smaller, and it is unlikely you would arrive here independently. Should you do so, a taxi to Plovdiv city centre will cost no more than 7.50 leva.

Varna is Bulgaria's best airport, though it is some way from the city centre. It is usually served by two flights a day from the capital. Cheap taxis abound, and the trip to the centre should cost about 20 leva.

Bourgas airport, another favourite destination of charter flights, is near the city centre, and served by at least one flight per day from Sofia. Budget airline Wizz Air flies daily from London in summer.

I need a taxi at the airport.	**Iskam taksi v letishte.**
How much?	**Kolko?**
That's too much!	**Mnogo e skarpo!**
Does this bus go to…	**Tozi li e avtobusart za…?**

B

BICYCLE HIRE

Cycling is not a popular pastime among Bulgarians; in urban areas it is unknown. In mountain resorts, however, such as Vitosha/Aleko, Bansko, Pamporovo and Borovets, you can hire mountain bikes at major hotels for around 20 leva per day. You will need to leave a credit card as a deposit. Big hotels in the main Black Sea resorts also hire out cycles. Hiring a motorbike is unheard of.

BUDGETING FOR YOUR TRIP

Still remarkably cheap by Western standards, prices in Bulgaria are nevertheless increasing fast. *(For exchange rates, see pages 120–1.)*

Transport. A standard cross-city taxi ride should not cost more than 20 leva, while bus tickets cost 0.70 leva in most cities. A one-way airline ticket from Sofia to Varna costs between 120 and 150 leva depending on the day of departure and time of the year.

Eating out. This can be as cheap or expensive as you wish. Good cheap cuisine is not difficult to find, but in Sofia and on the coast especially, you can just as easily spend a fortune. A top-class dinner in one of Sofia's five-star hotels will cost at least 100 leva per head, but a standard Bulgarian restaurant off Boulevard Vitosha will serve hearty portions of local fare for less than 10 leva per head.

C

CAMPING

Not exactly popular with locals, except when climbing in the mountains, camping in Bulgaria is not really recommended, as there is little provision for campers anywhere except at the Black Sea coast. Contact the Bulgarian Tourist Office in Sofia (tel: 02-987 97 78) for further information. Camping rough is illegal.

CAR HIRE

Hiring a car in Bulgaria is relatively expensive, with daily rates starting at around 120 leva. To get the best out of Bulgaria though, especially if you want to visit the Rila Monastery or any of the other sites off the beaten track, hiring a car for a day or two is essential.

All the major car-hire companies have offices throughout the country, including at Sofia and Varna airports, and cars can be hired from agencies at most big hotels. Petrol is cheap, though most roads, especially outside of major urban areas, are in poor condition. Driving at night can be extremely hazardous *(see also pages 112–13)*.

One option worth bearing in mind is to hire a car with a driver. The best way to do this is to approach a taxi driver in Sofia or any of the major towns and simply ask if he is available, then negotiate a price. It is unlikely that you will be refused, and you should be able to secure your man for around 100 leva per day, plus petrol and meals and accommodation.

CLIMATE

In general, Bulgaria's winters are bitterly cold, while summers range from warm to very hot. Spring and autumn tend to be very short and very wet. There are many regional variations. Along the Black Sea coast, for example, winters are more moderate than in Sofia, and summer temperatures can reach Mediterranean heights. The mountains receive large amounts of snow, which may remain until June in some areas. The Danube plain is the country's driest region.

The table below shows the average maximum and minimum tempratures for Sofia. Along the Black Sea, the average January temperature range is -1–6°C (30–43°F) and the July temperature ranges between 19°C (66°F) and 30°C (86°F).

	J	F	M	A	M	J	J	A	S	O	N	D
°C	-4	-3	1	5	10	14	16	15	11	8	3	-2
	2	4	10	16	21	24	27	26	22	17	9	4
°F	25	27	34	41	50	57	61	59	52	46	37	28
	36	39	50	61	70	75	81	79	72	63	48	39

CLOTHING

Winters are cold, summers are warm, so dress accordingly. Expect rain at any time of year. Bulgarians have few hang-ups about clothing, but you should note that most local women will cover their heads before entering churches and cathedrals; visitors are under no obligation to do the same, however. If invited into a Bulgarian home you should remove – or at least offer to remove – your footwear.

CRIME AND SAFETY

If you keep your nose clean, Bulgaria is as safe a country as they come. Stray dogs carrying rabies pose a threat to travellers in Sofia. Beggars can be pushy in major tourist areas, especially in Sofia around the Sheraton Hotel and TZUM department store, but they are rarely aggressive. You should keep your valuables safe, however, especially when riding public transport. The tram routes to and from the station in Sofia are notorious for pickpockets, as are the buses on the coast. The Black Sea's busiest beaches are also a haven for thieves.

Where is the police station?	**Kade e naybliskiyat politseyski uchastek?**
My ... has been stolen. passport/handbag/wallet	**Otkradnaha mi... passport/chantata/portfela.**
Stop thief!	**Spri! Krazhba!**
Help!	**Pomisht!**

CUSTOMS AND ENTRY REQUIREMENTS

Citizens of the EU and EEA countries (Switzerland, Norway, Iceland) may enter Bulgaria visa free and stay for as long as they please. Americans, Australians, Canadians and New Zealanders may all enter visa free, but are limited to stays of 30 days. Citizens of almost all other countries need to acquire a visa from a Bulgarian Embassy abroad before travelling. For a full list of Bulgarian consulates and visa requirements, visit the Bulgarian Foreign Ministry's website at <www.mfg.government.bg>.

Visas can no longer be purchased at the border so must be procured at a Bulgarian consulate abroad before entering the country.

Should you wish to extend your stay beyond 30 days, you will need to present yourself at a local police station to obtain a visa extension.

Customs regulations are standard, and duty-free allowances follow international norms: two bottles of alcohol, 200 cigarettes or 50 cigars or 25 grams of tobacco are the personal limits. Since Bulgaria joined the EU in January 2007, there are no limits for those travelling to and from EU countries. Cash in excess of €10,000 (or equivalent) must be declared on entry. You may not take more than 2,000 leva out of the country in cash.

D

DISABLED TRAVELLERS

Pushed by the EU, Bulgaria is making giant strides towards better accommodating disabled travellers, but getting around the country remains difficult for all but the fittest. Sofia is leading the way, installing rudimentary wheelchair ramps in many public squares, museums, tourist attractions and metro stations. The Black Sea coast is also rich in hotels that would not hesitate to accommodate disabled guests. The mountain resorts and other cities are less accessible.

DRIVING

Bulgarians drive on the right, though in the countryside such rules are often seen as being loose, at best. If you intend to bring your car to Bulgaria make sure you have your national driving licence with you, and proof of international insurance cover (a green card). Those who have forgotten can buy insurance at the border. You will have a stamp placed in your passport showing that you arrived by car. If you attempt to leave by any other method of transport you will have to explain what you have done with the car.

Driving in major cities is no better or worse than in any other country and roads are generally fine. Things are very different outside of the cities. There are only two real highways in the country, part of the

Sofia–Plovdiv and Sofia–Pravets routes (both have tolls) and most other inter-urban roads have single lanes. Roads in general are poorly sign-posted, so be sure to have a good map. Road surfaces are poor, and be particularly careful at night, as few highways have lights. Be especially wary of random Gypsy carts and stray animals when passing through villages. The speed limit is 60km/h (37mph) in the cities, 80km/h (40mph) on the open road and 120km/h (75mph) on the two highways. Bulgarians, though, appear not to be aware of these limits.

petrol/diesel	**benzin/dizel**
Full tank, please.	**Napelnete dogore, molya.**
My car has broken down.	**Stana avariya.**
There's been an accident.	**Stana katastrofa.**
Can I park here?	**Moga li da ostavya kolata si tuk?**

E

ELECTRICITY

Bulgaria uses the 200 volts AC system, like much of continental Europe. Visitors from the UK and the US will need an adaptor.

EMBASSIES AND CONSULATES

Australia (consulate): 37 ul Trakia, Sofia, tel: (02) 946 13 34.
Canada 11 ul Assen Zlatarov, Sofia, tel: (02) 943 37 04.
South Africa 1 ul Al Gendov, Sofia, tel: (02) 971 34 25.
UK 9 ul Moskovska, Sofia, tel: (02) 933 92 22.
US 1 ul Saborna, tel: (02) 937 51 00.
There is no New Zealand Embassy in Bulgaria.

I want to contact my embassy.	**Iskam da napravia vruska smoeto posolstvo.**

EMERGENCIES

Ambulance: **150**
Police: **166**
Fire Brigade: **160**

Fire!	**Pozhar!**
Help!	**Pomisht!**
Call the...	**Molya, povikayte...**
police /ambulance/	**politsiya/lineyka/**
fire brigade	**pozharnata**

G

GAY AND LESBIAN TRAVELLERS

Gay sex was decriminalised after pressure from the EU. Homosexual practices among consenting adults over the age of 21 are legal, but Bulgaria remains homophobic. There is a nascent gay scene in Sofia, but it is small and well hidden. The Bulgarian Gay Organization operates in Sofia (tel: 02-987 68 72; <www.bgogemini.org>).

GETTING THERE

With the entry of budget airlines to the local market, Bulgaria has become more accessible than ever. Wizz Air flies from London to Sofia and Bourgas, while Sky Europe flies from Budapest to Varna and Bourgas.

Package tours

For visitors from the UK and Ireland the best and cheapest way to get to Bulgaria remains as part of a package, either to the mountain resorts of Bansko, Borovets or Pamporovo, or to the Black Sea. Even if you intend travelling independently, a package deal with charter flight, hotel and half-board can often be cheaper than a scheduled flight to Sofia, especially if you can book well in advance or at the last minute. UK tour operators who feature Bulgaria include Thomson, Crystal and Balkan Holidays.

By air
Flying is the best way to reach Bulgaria. There are direct scheduled flights to Sofia from Amsterdam, Athens, Berlin, Brussels, Budapest, Bucharest, Copenhagen, Damascus, Dubai, Frankfurt, Istanbul, Kiev, Lisbon, London, Madrid, Milan, Paris, Prague, Rome, St Petersburg, Vienna, Warsaw and Zurich. The state airline, Balkan, went bankrupt a few years ago and split into a number of smaller airlines, including Bulgaria Air and Hemus Air. Prices for most scheduled flights tend to be high, but should come down soon thanks to pressure from the discount airlines Wizz Air and Sky Europe, both now serving Bulgaria.

You can fly direct to Varna from Budapest, Copenhagen, Frankfurt, London, Munich and Prague, though bear in mind most of these flights are charters and are strictly seasonal. Likewise, ski charters fly in winter to Plovdiv from London and Manchester.

By train
You can enter Bulgaria by train from Romania (at Ruse from Bucharest, or at Vidin from Craiova); from Greece (at Kulata, from Athens and Salonika); from Turkey (at Kapitan Andreevo, from Istanbul). There is also a daily train to Sofia from Budapest that runs via Belgrade.

By road
There are numerous land crossings into Bulgaria from Romania, Turkey, Greece, Macedonia and Serbia-Montenegro. The busiest, and those most likely to be used to Western visitors and their cars, are at Ruse (from Romania), Kapitan Andreevo (from Turkey), Kalat (from Greece) and Kalotina (from Serbia-Montenegro).

H

HEALTH AND MEDICAL CARE

There are no specific health risks particular to Bulgaria, though you should take out adequate health insurance cover before departing as a matter of course. Hepatitis A inoculation is sometimes recommended if you are travelling widely in the country. General standards of health care are fine, though, and in an emergency telephone **150** for an ambulance. Emergency medical treatment is free, but you may have to pay for some medicines, and you should tip the doctor and nurses. If it is private medical care you are after, head for **IMC Medical** in Sofia, at 28 ul Gogol, tel: (02) 944 93 26.

Tap water is safe to drink, though the low cost of the bottled variety means that very few people actually do. Mosquitoes are a problem all over the country during summer, so insect repellent is a must. Stray dogs can be a problem in Sofia and Varna; bites are more common in summer than winter. Though outbreaks of rabies are rare, should you be bitten, go to a hospital immediately for a rabies injection.

chemist	**apteka**
dentist	**zubolekar**
doctor	**lekar**
I need a doctor who speaks English.	**Iskam lekar Angliski.**

HOLIDAYS

Bulgaria has a number of public holidays, and Easter is the biggest celebration of all. Orthodox Easter, the date of which is set using the old, Julian calendar, usually falls a week after Catholic and Protestant Easter. In Bulgaria, only Easter Sunday and Monday are considered holidays. Good Friday is a normal working day. Easter can sometimes fall after 1 May. Note that if a holiday falls on a weekend, so be it. The Western practice of taking the next working day off is not yet a Bulgarian one.

1 January	New Year's Day
3 May	Liberation Day
April/May	Orthodox Easter
1 May	Labour Day
6 May	Army Day
24 May	Education Day (in honour of Sts Cyril and Methodius)
6 September	Reunion Day
22 September	Independence Day
24, 25, 26 December	Christmas

For more details on local religious and other festivals, *see page 96.*

L

LANGUAGE

Bulgarian is a Slavic language spoken by the entire population. Closely related to Serbian, Croatian and Slovene, it resembles Russian due to its use of the Cyrillic script, which can appear impenetrable to the visitor. We advise you strongly to spend an hour or two learning the Cyrillic characters, as few signs – even in Sofia and on the coast – appear in Latin script, and knowledge of the alphabet will save you both time and stress. To assist with navigation, we have included the Cyrillic for main locations in the Where to Go chapter.

English is widely spoken along the Black Sea coast and in the ski resorts, less so in urban areas (even Sofia) and not at all in the countryside. German will get you further, while Russian, though spoken to an extent by most Bulgarians of a certain age, is met with derision.

The Bulgarian Cyrillic alphabet

А	а	**a** as in b**a**th
Б	б	**b** as in **b**oat
В	в	**v** as in **v**an
Г	г	**g** as in **g**reat
Д	д	**d** as in **d**ead
Е	е	**e** as in l**e**t
Ж	ж	**s** as in mea**s**ure
З	з	**z** as in **z**ip
И	и	**ee** as in m**ee**t
Й	й	**yee** as in **yee**
К	к	**k** as in **k**appa
Л	л	**l** as in **l**ook
М	м	**m** as in **m**an
Н	н	**n** as in **n**ever
О	о	**a** as in b**a**ll
П	п	**p** as in **p**ower
Р	р	**r** as in **r**un
С	с	**s** as in **S**pain
Т	т	**t** as in **t**ell
У	у	**oo** as in b**oo**t
Ф	ф	**f** as in **f**ever
Х	х	**h** as in **h**ot
Ч	ч	**ch** as in **ch**at
Ц	ц	**ts** as in le**ts**
Ш	ш	**sh** as in **sh**op
Щ	щ	**sht** – represents two consonants like -**shed** in ma**shed**.
Ъ	ъ	a little similar to the **a** in England
	ь	no sound; softens the preceding consonant
Ю	ю	**you** as in **you**
Я	я	**ya** as in **ya**nk

Some useful words

yes/no	**da/nyet**	good morning	**dobro utro**
please	**molya**	good afternoon	**dobar dan**
thank you	**mersi**	good night	**dobar vecher**
excuse me	**izvinete me**	goodbye	**dovizdhanay**

Days of the week

Monday	**ponedelnik**	Friday	**petak**
Tuesday	**vtornik**	Saturday	**sobota**
Wednesday	**sryada**	Sunday	**nedelya**
Thursday	**chetvurtek**		

Numbers

one	**edin**	seventeen	**sedemnayset**
two	**dva**	eighteen	**asemnayset**
three	**tri**	nineteen	**devetnayset**
four	**chetiri**	twenty	**dvayset**
five	**pyet**	twenty-one	**dvayset i edin**
six	**shest**	twenty-two	**dvayset i dva**
seven	**sedem**	twenty-three	**dvayset i tri**
eight	**osem**	thirty	**triset**
nine	**devet**	forty	**chetiriset**
ten	**deset**	fifty	**pedeset**
eleven	**edinayset**	sixty	**shestdeset**
twelve	**dvanayset**	seventy	**sedemdeset**
thirteen	**trinayset**	eighty	**osemdest**
fourteen	**chetirinayset**	ninety	**devetdeset**
fifteen	**pyetnayset**	one hundred	**sto**
sixteen	**shestnayset**	one thousand	**hilyada**

M

MAPS

Most hotel concierges will be able to provide you with some kind of city or town map, but few are any good, as they are little more than vehicles for tacky advertisements. One exception is the *Sofia: To Know Where* map produced by the Bulgarian Tourist Board and available at most hotels. The best map of the whole country is produced by Kartografiya Eood, and can be found at most good international travel bookshops. The same company also produces excellent maps to the Pirin, Rila and Balkan mountain ranges, with all hiking routes and cabins well marked.

MEDIA

Local television tends to be poor, offering little more than imported rubbish dubbed into Bulgarian. Most hotels in Sofia, larger towns, the ski resorts and on the coast offer cable or satellite TV with BBC World and CNN as part of the programme package. You will find the English press at newsstands in five-star hotels, around the Sheraton, on Vitosha Boulevard, and at the airport. Kiosks at the Black Sea also stock foreign magazines and newspapers in season, though usually with a two- or three-day delay.

The *Sofia Echo*, a rather dry weekly newspaper, is the only English-language news publication. The online news agency Novinite <www.novinite.com> is a good source of local news in reasonably good English.

MONEY

Bulgaria's currency is the *lev*, plural *leva*. It is usually written in full (leva). Banknotes come in denominations of 200, 100, 50, 20, 10, 5, 2 and 1. You will also find 1 and 2 leva coins. One lev is worth 100 *stotinki*, coins which come in denominations of 50, 20, 10, 5, 2 and 1. The lev is pegged to the euro at the unforgettable rate of 1:1.92513;

£1 = 2.9 leva; US$1 = 1.6. Many services, especially taxis, can un-officially be paid for in euros – notes only, and do not expect change.

Changing money is best done inside a bank, though the fixed rate means that being fleeced is difficult. Never change money on the street. ATMs are ubiquitous, and Visa/MasterCard credit cards are accepted in hotels, restaurants and shops. Holders of American Express and Diners Club cards may struggle, however.

Traveller's cheques should always be changed inside a bank.

Where is the nearest bank?	**Znaete li kade tuk ima banka?**
I want to change…	**Iskam da smenya…**
some money	**liri**
some traveller's cheques	**tozi patnicheski chek**
The ATM has swallowed	**Bankomatet ne vrushta**
my card	**kartata mi**

OPENING HOURS

Government offices, banks and other institutions are usually open 8.30am–3pm, Mon–Fri, without pause for lunch. Museums have variable opening hours, which tend to be variations on 10am–6pm. Most museums close on Mondays, some on Sundays, too, and you may find, particularly in the countryside, that they are closed at lunchtime.

Shops and supermarkets are open Mon–Sat 9am–6pm, though many stay open later. Most shops in Sofia also open on Sunday.

P

POLICE

Police in our experience are helpful and friendly, though in most cases do not speak English. The police force shows little interest in foreign tourists, so unless you go looking for trouble or decide to drive at excessive speeds, you will have little to do with them. Should you need them in an emergency, shout loudly or dial 166.

| Where's the police station? | **Kade e nay bliskiyat politseyski uchastek?** |
| I've lost my... passport/luggage | **Zagubi si... pasport/bagash** |

POST OFFICES

Post offices can be found in most cities and towns, though if you are posting something abroad, it is best to do it from Sofia or Varna, or else your intended recipient could be waiting some time. The central post office in Sofia is at 6 ul Gurko, behind the Radisson Hotel, and is open Mon–Sat 7.30am–8pm. In Varna the main post office is at 36 bul Saborni, opposite the Cathedral of the Assumption, and is open Mon–Fri 7.30–8pm, Sat 7.30–1pm.

For urgent letters and packets, Mon–Sat, DHL have offices in most major cities. Call (02) 969 33 60 for DHL in Sofia.

| I want to send this by... airmail express | **Molya, tova pismo da bede... svezdushna poshta serza poshta** |

PUBLIC TRANSPORT

Taxis

Taxis in Bulgaria were once unregulated rip-offs, every single one. Now, thanks to legislation, all are metered, must provide all clients with a receipt, and in Sofia at least all have to be yellow. That is not to say that visitors are never fooled into paying too much; some are. But if you keep your wits about you and always use a taxi that clearly displays the name of the company it belongs to (Yellow Taxi 02-911 19; EuroTaxi 02-910 33; Sofia Taxi 02-974 47 47; OK Supertrans 02-973 21 21 in Sofia) you will find taxis astonishingly cheap. Don't expect operators or drivers to speak English, however, and you may like to ask your hotel concierge or restaurant waiter to order one for you.

Take me to this address.	**Kam [address], molya.**
Please stop here.	**Mozhe li da sprete tuk?**

Trains

Bulgaria's railway network is extensive, cheap and generally reliable, though somewhat slow. Even the rather optimistically named *InterCity* and *Expres* trains are gruelling. For example, the quickest of the five daily trains from Sofia to Varna takes a mind-numbing eight and a half hours. If you do wish to travel cross-country by train, it is best to do so at night, on a sleeper *(spalen)*, which offers good value and at least allows you to pass the hours unconscious.

Buying tickets can be a laborious process in Bulgaria; expect no help from ticket staff either. The best place to buy tickets is the office of Wasteels, to the left of the entrance to Sofia station.

How much is the fare to…?	**Kolko shte struva do…?**
I want a ticket to…	**Iskam edin bilet za…**
single (one way)	**ednoposochen bilet**
return (round trip)	**dvuposochen bilet**
first/second class	**perva klasa/ftora klasa**

Aeroplanes

Bulgaria has a good internal airline service, with the cities of Varna, Bourgas, Plovdiv, Gorna Orjahovica (Veliko Tarnovo) and

Ruse all served from Sofia. Domestic airline tickets sell for approximately 120–140 leva each way, depending on the season. Call Bulgaria Air (tel: 02-865 95 17/57) at Sofia airport for timetable and ticket information.

R

RELIGION

The vast majority of the Bulgarian population is Eastern Orthodox, similar in almost every way to the Orthodoxy practised in Russia, Romania, Serbia-Montenegro and Macedonia, though somewhat different from (and frequently at odds with) Greek Orthodoxy. There are also Muslim, Jewish and Catholic minorities.

Khan Boris, one of the first Bulgar leaders, declared Christianity the state religion in 865, partly in an attempt to appease the majority Slavs, most of whom had by then converted to Christianity. Many of the ethnic Bulgars at that stage remained pagans.

The Bulgarian Orthodox Church has had its own patriarch since 896, when Simeon the Great established the patriarchate as a bulwark against Byzantine influence over the country. The Bulgarian church subsequently became one of the great crusading influences over the Slavonic world as Simeon expanded his empire with the invention of the Cyrillic alphabet by two Salonika-based monks, Cyril and Methodius *(see page 16)*.

Under the Ottoman Yoke large numbers of Bulgarians (Gypsies in particular) converted to Islam, and with large numbers of Turks emigrating from Asia to Europe throughout the period, by the 1800s it is estimated that almost a third of the country's population was Muslim. After liberation, however, and especially after the Second Balkan War, huge numbers of Turks left Bulgaria. Today, around 700,000 ethnic Turks remain in Bulgaria.

Though the Communist regime was nominally atheist it nevertheless tolerated the Bulgarian Orthodox Church, and until the 1970s paid at least lip service to the notion of minority rights, before embarking on a fierce programme of Bulgarianisation. Turks either changed their names to sound Bulgarian or faced limited persecution.

Bulgaria's Jews suffered the most of all the minorities. Before World War II there were around 50,000 in Bulgaria, but in 1943 as many as 20,000 were rounded up by the pro-Nazi Bulgarian government of Bogdan Filov and all perished in the death camps. However, popular outrage at the atrocity from ordinary Bulgarians forced the government to rethink its policies, and it subsequently refused German demands to deport the remaining Jews held in camps inside Bulgaria. Following the war most Jews fled to Palestine, and now around 5,000 remain.

T

TELEPHONE, FAX AND EMAIL

The country code for Bulgaria is +359. The city code for Sofia is 02, and for Varna 052. Other important city codes include: Blagoevgrad 073, Bourgas 056, Plovdiv 032, Veliko Tarnovo 062. The first 0 in the city code is dropped when making an international call to Bulgaria. When dialling within Bulgaria the city code is used in full, unless you are dialling a number in the same city or area. To dial out of Bulgaria, dial 00, the country and city code, then the number.

You can dial internationally from most hotel rooms (at an extravagant cost) and most public phones also permit direct dialling. All public phones require a phonecard, available from newsstands and kiosks.

If you need to send or receive a fax, do so from a post office, as hotels charge well over the odds for the privilege.

Internet cafés are ubiquitous, and an increasing number of hotels also offer internet access via laptop plug-ins in rooms. The Bulgarian internet domain is <.bg>.

TIME DIFFERENCES

Bulgaria is two hours ahead of Greenwich Mean Time. The chart below shows the times in Bulgaria and various other cities.

New York	London	Jo'burg	**Sofia**	Sydney	Auckland
5am	10am	noon	**noon**	9pm	11pm

TIPPING

You are expected to tip waiters and waitresses in restaurants (though check your bill to ensure that service is not already included), domestic hotel staff and doormen. Note that in these cases a 10 percent tip is seen as obligatory, regardless of whether you have been happy with the service. Taxi drivers do not expect to be tipped, and you should do so only if you have taken a taxi on a particularly short journey, in order to make the ride worth the cabby's time and trouble.

TOILETS

There are few decent public toilets in Bulgaria. In Sofia the only public toilets we would recommend are in the TZUM shopping centre and in the basement of the Halite. In the mountains even restaurant and mountain retreat toilets can leave a lot to be desired, and many are of the common squat variety. You should bring your own toilet paper.

Where are the toilets?	**Kadye e toaletnata?**

TOURIST INFORMATION

Though Bulgaria no longer has an established tourist information office network abroad – a legacy of budget cuts – it has recently developed a good internal network of tourist information offices. Most towns and cities now have some kind of information office, the notable exception being Plovdiv.

Sofia: pl Sv Nedelya 1; tel/fax 02-987 97 78
Varna: bul Tzar Osvoboditel 36; tel/fax: 052-602 907
Veliko Tarnovo: pl Mayka Bulgaria

tourist information office	**touristicheska informaciya**
Do you have a map of Sofia?	**Imate li karta na Sofia?**
Are there any tours of the city?	**Provezhdat li se obikolki iz grada?**

WEBSITES

Discover Bulgaria, <www.discover-bulgaria.com>, is a useful site, covering the whole country, with both information and a hotel reservation service. Another good site that provides critical reviews of hotels, restaurants and bars in Sofia, as well as sights and events listings for the capital, is Sofia In Your Pocket: <www.inyourpocket.com>.

The Bulgarian National Tourist Office's official site, <www.bulgariatravel.org>, paints a rather rosy picture of even the dreariest Bulgarian towns, though it does provide good general information, and its skiing and hiking pages are very well done.

For news, try the English-language Sofia-based news agency Novinite: <www.novinite.com>.

YOUTH HOSTELS

There are no IYH-affiliated youth hostels in Bulgaria. There are a few independent places in various towns, but you should avoid them unless you are on a really tight budget. Private rooms in local houses (most railway stations are full of old ladies offering rooms and board) are the best budget accommodation option.

Recommended Hotels

Good accommodation in Bulgaria has always been easy to find, though value for money was for a long time thin on the ground. Now that market forces have replaced central planning and hotel staff actually have to work for a living, you will find high standards of customer service everywhere. The accommodation scene is still dominated by high-rise hotels built during the 1960s and 1970s, but almost all of these have now been privatised, and in most cases renovated. A number of cheaper, smaller hotels have also opened, offering bed-and-breakfast, while private apartments, either with the owner present or not, are also popular, especially in the cities.

Turning up at a hotel on spec in any of the ski or beach resorts will result in you paying far in excess of what package tourists pay. If possible, you should arrange accommodation in these resorts through an agent, either from home or in Sofia. Try Alexander Tour in Sofia, 44 ul Pop Bogomil, tel: (02) 983 33 22, <www.alexandertour.com>.

Also note that given the number of very similar hotels in Sunny Beach and Golden Sands we have not listed individual establishments for those places. All are well used by Western tour groups and all are adequate if not outstanding.

€€€	more than 200 leva
€€	100–200 leva
€	under 100 leva

SOFIA

Art'Otel €€ *44 ul William Gladstone, tel: (02) 980 60 00, email: <arthotel@fog-bg.net>.* Stylish hotel just off bul Vitosha. Just 19 elegant rooms, all uniquely decorated and offering good-value accommodation. The Tower suite is the best.

City Best Western €€ *6 ul Stara Planina, tel: (02) 915 15 00, <www.bwcityhotel.com>.* Decent accommodation just north of the city centre. Rooms are a little on the anonymous side, but this hotel represents very good value. Only 36 rooms, so reservations essential.

Grand Hotel Sofia €€€ *1 ul Gurko, tel: (02) 811 08 00, <www. grandhotelsofia.bg>.* Opposite the National Theatre, this outstanding hotel is classy from beginning to end. Smartly dressed doormen welcome you in, friendly reception staff meet and greet you, while the sheer opulence of the rooms will ensure your stay is a spacious, pleasurable and luxurious one.

Hilton Sofia €€€ *1 bul Bulgaria, tel: (02) 933 50 00, <www.hilton. com>.* This homage to glass was built in 2000 and is well positioned next to the National Palace of Culture (NDK). Even the standard rooms are large, let alone the executive rooms and suites. Excellent restaurant. This is one of the best Hiltons there is. 245 standard rooms.

Holiday Inn Sofia €€ *111 bul Alexandar Malinov, tel: (02) 807 07 07, <www.holidayinn-bg.com>.* The newest hotel in town. Although the location in the Sofia business park is not the best for tourists, the quality is high and prices are surprisingly low, especially at weekends when the conference crowd is absent. There's a huge swimming pool and fitness centre. A good choice for those with their own car.

Kempinski Hotel Zografski €€€ *100 bul James Bouchier, tel: (02) 969 22 22, <www.kempinski.com>.* Situated just outside the centre of Sofia in a pleasantly leafy suburb, the Kempinski is one of the oldest high-rises in Sofia, built by Japanese businessmen in the 1970s. It is now part of the Kempinski hotel chain; fully five star though its grandeur is somewhat faded. The city's best Japanese restaurant is in the basement. Excellent sport and fitness complex. 428 rooms.

Meg-Lozenets €€ *84 ul Krum Popov, tel: (02) 965 18 70.* Newish three-star hotel offering good-value, tasteful rooms. In a nice, residential area close to the National Palace of Culture (NDK). 86 rooms.

Radisson SAS Grand Hotel €€€ *4 pl Narodno Sabranie, tel: (02) 933 43 43, <www.radissonsas.com>.* This shining glass edifice is located close to the Alexander Nevski Cathedral. The Radisson SAS is splendour and luxury throughout. Fine rooms, and five-star service. Also at the hotel are the highly recommended Flanagans Irish pub and the upmarket Panorama BBQ restaurant *(see page 137)*. 136 rooms.

Scotty's €€ *11 ul Ezarkh Iosif, tel: (02) 983 67 77, <www.geocities. com/scottysboutiquehotel>*. A renovated townhouse offers good value accommodation in a central location. The attic room (Auckland – all 16 rooms are named after a city around the world), with its sloping ceilings, wooden beams, nooks and crannies, has real character.

Serdika € *2 bul Yanko Sakazov, tel: (02) 846 54 85*. Thoroughly renovated hotel in the heart of town close to the Vasili Levski monument. Rooms are basic but clean and bright. The Serdika is about the cheapest of Sofia's centrally located hotels. 70 rooms.

Sheraton Sofia Hotel Balkan €€€ *5 pl Sveta Nedelya, tel: (02) 980 65 41, <www.starwoodhotels.com/sheraton>*. The oldest of the city's five-star hotels and still the No. 1 choice of travellers for whom location is everything. A living piece of the city's history first, the Sheraton stands imposingly on Sofia's central square and has all the amenities and luxury you would expect of this hotel chain. 173 rooms.

Sveta Sofia €€ *18 ul Pirotska, tel: (02) 981 26 34, email: <sveta sofia@abv.bg>*. Situated on Sofia's one pedestrian street, you'll love the location and the 18 elegant rooms, though the noise from the lively street below may deter families with young children.

AROUND THE COUNTRY

BANSKO

Bansko €€€ *17 ul Glazne, tel: (0749) 880 55*. Large hotel a short walk from the centre of Bansko with indoor swimming pool and fitness centre, and large, comfortable, individually furnished rooms. Also has one of the best *mehana* in town.

Chateau Vaptsarov €€€ *23 ul Solun, tel: (0749) 882 81*. The stunning Chateau has large, comfortable rooms with satellite TV and internet access, plus a large health complex with sauna, steam bath, hot tub and massage. Price includes daily transport to the gondola lift.

Evelina Palace €€ *98 ul Ikonom Chuchulain 34, tel: (0749) 864 30, <www.evelinapalace.com>.* Large bright rooms and a wonderful swimming pool, complete with separate children's area, make this new but attractive hotel a hit with families. Staff are the friendliest in town and the buffet breakfast is superb.

Kempinski Grand Arena €€€ *ul Pirin, tel: (0749) 888 88, <www.kempinski-bansko.com>.* Next to the gondola lift, the location of this huge, luxurious hotel could not be better. Nor could the service, staff, rooms or restaurants. Set over five interconnected buildings, this is one of the few newly built Bansko hotels that have genuinely tried to blend in with their mountainous surroundings. The spa and wellness centre, with a huge indoor pool, will keep non-skiers occupied.

Pirin €€€ *bul Tsar Simeon, tel: (0749) 880 51.* This historic hotel close to Bansko's central square was recently fully renovated and is now one of the best in the resort. Indoor swimming pool, fitness centre, sauna, solarium, steam room and excellent *mehana*.

BOROVETS

Note that in Borovets and Pamporovo the streets have no name.

Rila €€€ *tel: (0750) 324 41.* For many years the monolithic Rila Hotel *was* Borovets, and it remains very much a resort within a resort. Renovated a couple of years ago, it now has an indoor swimming pool, fitness centre and kindergarten. Rooms are large but spartan.

Samokov €€€ *tel: (0750) 323 06.* Enormous hotel dating from 1990, close to the Yastrabets gondola, offering large, comfortable rooms, a swimming pool, fitness centre, shops and a very good restaurant. Large, characterless rooms, but great views.

Vila Stresov €€€ *tel: (02) 980 42 92, <www.villastresov.com>.* Stunning, Swiss-style villa in a lovely setting. Rooms are luxurious, and there is a sauna, Jacuzzi and leafy garden. The best accommodation in Borovets, though it comes at a price. Bookings are made through the villa's Sofia office, or online at the villa's website.

Yastrabets €€€ *tel: (0750) 322 12*. A less plush but reasonably good-value hotel at the foot of the Yastrabets ski runs, close to the gondola lift. The terrace here is the resort's most popular – weather permitting.

PAMPOROVO

Extreme €€ *tel: (0309) 598 98, <www.hotel-extreme.com>*. Despite the name, you do not have to be an extreme snowboarder to stay at this elegant contemporary hotel. Rooms are large, the restaurant is very good and the bar is one of the resort's liveliest. There's après-ski massage and relaxation in an onsite spa centre too.

Finlandia €€€ *tel: (0309) 583 67*. The Finlandia has been built with taste and no shortage of style. It has 54 comfortable rooms and apartments, and a wide variety of facilities. Great buffet breakfast included.

Malina Village €€ *tel: (0309) 583 88*. Cosy two-level chalets in a remote part of the resort offer a back-to-nature way to enjoy Pamporovo. Most chalets have en-suite saunas, and the village has a restaurant.

Mourgavets €€ *tel: (0309) 583 10*. Ugly as hell but as comfortable as heaven, the recently renovated Mourgavets offers terrific views from its upper floors and is very good value for money.

Pamporovo €€€ *tel: (0309) 581 22*. Once the best hotel in the Bulgarian mountains, the Pamporovo has everything from an Irish pub to a Turkish bath, as well as enormous rooms with views to die for.

PLOVDIV

Bulgaria €€ *13 bul Evtimil, tel: (032) 63 35 99; <www.hotel bulgaria.net>*. Plush, historic hotel in the heart of the city, with large but not luxurious rooms, a casino and a trendy terrace café.

Hebros €€ *51A ul Konstantin Stoilov, tel: (032) 26 01 80, <www. hebros-hotel.com>.* A National Revival-style house with period rooms that cleverly disguise the modern amenities, all added in 1999 when the hotel was totally renovated.

Noviz €€ *55 bul Ruski, tel: (032) 63 12 81, <www.noviz.ttg.bg/ hotel>.* Small but reasonably smart, if old-fashioned, four-star hotel opposite Budjarnik Park. All bathrooms have a tub – a definite plus in this part of the world – and prices include a good breakfast in the hotel's restaurant.

Novotel Plovdiv €€€ *2 ul Zlatyu Boyadzhiev, tel: (032) 93 44 44, <www.novotelpdv.bg>.* Situated on the northern bank of the Maritsa River, this sparkling five-star is Plovdiv's best hotel. Overlooking the gorgeous slopes of the Rhodopes, it is close to the trade fair grounds and is often full during May and September. Reservations are essential.

Trimontium Princess €€€ *2 ul Kapitan Raicho, tel: (032) 60 50 00, <www.trimontium-princess.com>.* Even people who do not stay here will see it: the grand, classically designed hotel dominates pl Tsentralen. The hotel casino is a favourite with visiting businessmen. Rooms are enormous, though the furniture betrays faded grandeur.

VELIKO TARNOVO

Arbanasi Palace €€€ *Arbanasi, tel: (062) 301 76.* Luxurious and understandably expensive hotel on a small side road leading from the village museum of Arbanasi, a 10-minute drive from Veliko Tarnovo. The bathrooms are bigger than most Bulgarian apartments, and the view from the terrace towards Veliko Tarnovo is nothing short of wondrous. From riding school to Roman bath – everything you could ever wish for is here.

Grand Hotel Veliko Tarnovo €€ *2 ul Al Panchev, tel: (062) 60 10 00.* Probably a lovely hotel once, the Grand is today not quite so grand as it would like to claim. Though the communal areas are all fine, and the sports club and swimming pool very good, some of the rooms are positively grotty. The views of the valley and the river are what you pay for.

Premier €€ *1 ul Sava Penev, tel: (062) 61 55 55.* Best hotel in Veliko Tarnovo itself, with rooms offering great views of the valley and the rest of the town. All rooms have internet access and large bathrooms. Two rooms are fitted out for use by disabled travellers.

Tsaravets €€ *23 ul Chitalishtna, tel: (0626) 01 885, <www.tsaravets hotel.com>.* This is a delightful hotel, situated on a quiet street in the heart of old Veliko Tarnovo. Originally a merchant's house, and built in 1891, it has been completely refurbished, yet all of the rooms remain elegantly and classically furnished. The high ceilings are wonderful, as are the views from almost all of the rooms.

THE COAST

NESSEBUR

Aquamarin €€ *3 ul Krajbrezna, tel: (0554) 4 33 60, <www.bourgas. org/aquamarin>.* Lovely little hotel on the northern tip of Old Nessebur. Rooms are a little basic, but the views out towards Sunny Beach are excellent. Great seafood restaurant, too.

Bora €€ *7 ul Slavianska, tel: (0554) 4 22 25.* Small, family-run hotel and restaurant in the centre of the Nessebur peninsula, next to the only working church in the old town. Luxuriously furnished rooms are often full in high season; best to reserve well ahead.

Mistral €€ *22 ul Khan Krum, tel: (0554) 77 41.* Modern, medium-sized hotel in the newer part of Nessebur, five minutes' walk from the town's main beach. Rooms are airy and well sized and an on-site sports centre offers a Jacuzzi, hydromassage and sauna.

Monte Kristo €€€ *5 ul Venera, tel: (0554) 4 20 55, email: <monte cristo@infotel.bg>.* In the heart of Old Nessebur the small, family run Monte Kristo is one of the best hotels on the coast. A fabulous restaurant only adds to the charm.

Old Nessebar €€ *12 ul Aheloy, tel: (0554) 438 50, <www.bourgas. org/oldnessebar>.* Delightful hotel situated in a gorgeous old house, recently renovated to include good-sized apartments and rooms. The views out to sea are sensational.

VARNA

Antik €€ *10 ul Ohrid, tel: (052) 63 21 67.* Varna's best kept secret: a smart little family-run hotel offering great-value rooms, all with small en-suite bathrooms and an excellent breakfast, just minutes from the station and the centre of town.

Aqua €€ *12 ul Devnya, tel: (052) 63 13 89, <www.aquahotels. com>.* This large, modern hotel opposite the railway station is popular with tour groups, and in high-season it can often be full. The suites are great value. Reservations recommended.

Capitol €€€ *40 ul Petko Karavelov, tel: (052) 68 80 00, <www. capitol.bg>.* Probably the classiest hotel in Varna itself, the Capitol offers large, stylish rooms and a splendid restaurant in a location close to the entrance of the municipal beach.

Grand Hotel Varna €€€ *St Elias Complex, Sv Konstantin, tel: (052) 36 10 89, <www.saintelias.bg>.* The best hotel on the coast is actually outside of Varna, in the satellite beach resort of Sv Konstantin, a 10-minute drive from the centre of the city. Every luxury is on offer in the 296 rooms and 35 suites, while there are indoor and outdoor pools, too. The beach is a short walk away.

Odessos €€€ *1 bul Slivnitsa, tel: (052) 60 81 85.* Enormous hotel on the seafront, at the entrance to the sea gardens, most rooms having great sea views. A little rundown and perhaps overpriced, rooms are still good and the location cannot be bettered.

Reverence €€ *58 bul Osmi Primorski Polk, tel: (052) 63 18 31, <www.reverence.bg.com>.* Small, quiet and welcoming hotel on one of Varna's main boulevards. Trendy terrace/bistro attracts some of the smartest people in town.

Recommended Restaurants

If Bulgarian cuisine itself offers little beyond the standard Balkan meat-and-cabbage-fest, portions tend to be huge, and there are always enough international restaurants to fill the breach so that finding good food should never be difficult. Eating out is increasingly popular with locals, and most of the places listed here will be full at weekends: it is always best to make a reservation. Prices can be high in the best restaurants.

Note that we have not listed individual restaurants for the ski resorts of Borovets and Pamporovo, nor for the seaside resorts of Golden Sands and Sunny Beach, for the reason that in the former almost all visitors eat in their hotels, while at the seaside restaurants come and go so quickly that individual listings (especially in resorts that have no street names) are pointless.

€€€€	more than 50 leva per head
€€€	25–50 leva
€€	10–25 leva
€	under 10 leva

SOFIA

Bai Gencho €€ *15 ul Dondulkov*. As famous for its wine collection as its food, Bai Gencho – a traditional Bulgarian restaurant – is easy to find on Dondulkov, a short walk towards the opera from TZUM. Five shops of the same name sell a great range of wines at various locations around Sofia.

Beyond the Alley, Behind the Cupboard (Otvud Aleyata, Zad Shkafa) €€€ *31 ul Budapeshta, tel: (02) 983 55 45, <www.beyond-the-alley.com>*. Probably the most famous restaurant in Sofia, and not without reason. Slightly off the beaten track along a dark, nondescript side street, this is one place well worth seeking out for top fusion cuisine in a super villa setting.

Bravo € *12 ul Aksakov, tel: (02) 981 49 16*. Bravo is a bright and breezy pizzeria serving top-quality, cheap-as-you-like pizzas in a central location. A few other so-called pizzerias in Sofia would do well to take lessons in pizza-making from these people. Summer terrace.

Café Lavazza €€€ *13 bul Vitosha, tel: (02) 987 34 33*. Just about the trendiest place in Sofia, Café Lavazza has everything going for it, most notably the people-watching location at the Sheraton end of bul Vitosha. The terrace and upstairs levels serve coffee and cakes all day, while from 7pm the rear of the ground floor turns into one of the city's best Italian restaurants.

Flanagans €€€ *4 pl Narodno Sobranie (Radisson SAS Sofia), tel: (02) 933 47 40*. A winner from the Radisson SAS, this Irish pub serves Guinness, pies and all-day breakfasts to ex-pats, visitors and Bulgarian Irish wannabes. Live music most weekend nights.

Fox & Hound €€ *34 ul Angel Kanchev, tel: (02) 980 74 27*. English pub and restaurant serving good food to a smart, trendy ex-pat and local crowd. Find it on a side street just behind bul Vitosha.

Kashtata €€ *4 ul Verila, tel: (02) 952 08 30*. Just about the most popular Bulgarian restaurant in the city, Kashtata (The Little House) has been around for years and is always full. Best to reserve ahead.

Krim €€ *17 ul Slavyanska, tel: (02) 981 06 66*. Bulgarian and Russian dishes have been served to the rich and famous at Krim for as long as anyone can remember. Some patrons have waited as long for their main courses.

Panorama €€€€ *1000 bul James Bouchier (Kempinksi Hotel Zografski), tel: (02) 969 24 40*. The best views in Sofia – the Panorama sits on the top floor of the Kempinski Hotel – come at a price, but the food is good enough to warrant the extravagance.

Panorama BBQ €€€€ *pl Narodno Subranie (Radisson SAS Sofia), tel: (02) 933 43 34*. The Radisson SAS's showpiece, and they have every right to be proud of it. Inventive salads complement the great steaks, while the outside setting offers respite from the Sofia heat on summer evenings.

Pri Yafata € *40 ul Raiko Alexiev, tel: (02) 971 30 78.* Excellent Bulgarian food served all day for tired shoppers and tourists in a corner location just off bul Vitosha. Cheerful staff and cheerfully cheap prices.

Rouge €€€ *17 ul Lyuben Karavelov, tel: (02) 986 48 76.* Top fusion cuisine at surprisingly sensible prices. The decor is modern and inventive, and the food is prepared by a chef who likes to experiment with new and interesting flavours. Reservations needed at weekends.

Seasons €€€€ *1 bul Bulgaria (Hilton Sofia), tel: (02) 933 50 62.* Few Hiltons in the world can boast a restaurant to match Seasons in the consistent quality of its food. For those who can afford it, a visit will be a highlight of a stay in Sofia. International and Bulgarian dishes rub shoulders on the menu.

Uno Enoteca €€€ *bul Vasili Levski 45, tel: (02) 981 43 72, <www.uno-sofia.com>.* This is Sofia's best Italian restaurant, where experimental seafood dishes dominate a wonderfully succinct menu. The elegant dining room is abandoned by diners in summer for the cool air of the covered garden.

AROUND THE COUNTRY

BANSKO

Most of Bansko's hotels and guest houses have on-site mehanas – *local restaurants – almost all of which are good. The best is the one at the Hotel Bansko at 17 ul Glazne.*

Baryakova Mehana € *ul Velyan Ognev 3, tel: (0749) 844 82.* Legendary *mehana* in the heart of Bansko's Old Town that comes into its own during the winter when open fires and cheap-as-you-like, huge portions of local dishes are served to locals and tourists enjoying the accompanying music.

Come Prima €€€€ *98 ul Pirin (Kempinski Grand Arena), tel: (0749) 888 88.* If the *mehanas* of Bansko get too much, try this small, exquisite restaurant at the Kempinski. Decorated in imperial, turn of the 19th-century style, the ever-changing menu is a culinary tour of the Mediterranean.

Dedo Pene €€ *ul Bujnov., tel: (0749) 883 48.* Probably Bansko's best-known restaurant, this place is located in the centre of town in a building dating from 1820, and offers a boisterous Bansko experience to the tour groups who flock here. There is a small hotel upstairs.

Obetsanovata Kushta €€ *pl Vazrazhdane, tel: (0749) 822 36.* Perhaps the oldest *mehana* in Bansko, this place will happily serve you an entire pig on a spit if you give them 48 hours notice. There are simple grilled meats and local dishes for the less adventurous.

Sharkova Kashta € *ul Peti Oktomvri, tel: (0749) 850 24.* Set in an attractive house and serving seafood alongside the traditional Bansko dishes, Sharkova is a cut above the average Bansko *mehana* and dirt cheap to boot.

PLOVDIV

Alafrangite €€ *17 ul Kiril Nektariev, tel: (032) 26 95 95.* Delightful restaurant set in a beautiful National Revival-period house in Old Plovdiv. Well-prepared and presented traditional Bulgarian meals served by staff who, for once, really appear to care. Chamber music is played in the lovely courtyard most evenings during the summer.

Chevermeto €€ *4 ul Dondukov, tel: (032) 62 86 05.* Great *mehana* serving some less common Bulgarian dishes, including lamb's liver with fresh herbs and *drob*, a kind of lamb pâté made with parts of the animal that would otherwise not be eaten.

Loven Park €€ *10 ul Yasna Polyana, tel: (032) 44 20 90.* Loven Park serves international cuisine of an excellent standard in a great spot away from the centre of the city, close to the zoo. Tremendously popular during the summer with locals.

Puldin €€€ *3 ul Knjaz Tsereletev, tel: (032) 63 17 20.* The best, most historic restaurant in Plovdiv (and probably the most expensive) is located in the heart of Old Town. Recently renovated it retains its original charm. Local dishes predominate; try the *chuksa banitsa* (peppers stuffed with feta cheese), a real treat. Or you can take the Puldin salad, a showcase platter featuring a number of Bulgarian salads. Garden in the summer.

VELIKO TARNOVO

Captain Cook €€ *ul Nezavisimost, no phone.* Ignore the cheesy name and instead enjoy some fine seafood at this enormous restaurant. A small terrace on the pavement outside fills up quickly in summer. The Captain Cook is the sister establishment of an even larger restaurant on the coast at Golden Sands.

Izvora Taverna €€€ *Arbanasi, tel: (0626) 01 205.* Located close to the Village Museum of Arbanasi, this is one of the best traditional restaurants in Bulgaria. It offers just about every Bulgarian dish imaginable, all served by staff in traditional dress, in a garden complete with fountains, ponds and playgrounds for children. The barbequed lamb dishes are particularly recommended.

Mehana Gurko €€ *33 ul Gurko, tel: (062) 62 78 38.* The best of Veliko Tarnovo's *mehanas* is often full with coach parties, so make sure you reserve a table beforehand. It's all genuine, home-cooked Bulgarian cuisine, though you may have a devil of a time finding the place, on a tiny side street off ul Rakovski. It's worth the hunt, though.

Mustang €€ *pl Mayka Bulgaria.* A long-standing local and tourist favourite (part of a Bulgaria-wide chain) serving fast-food versions of Bulgarian classics. The terrace and views are what bring the crowds in, with the Tsaravets visible from the tables closest to the entrance.

NESSEBUR

Andromeda €€ *ul Ivan Alexander, tel: (05...* fish and the views at this good-value restaura... Impeccably prepared seafood a world away fro... traps that litter the area.

Golden Fleece €€ *6 ul Rusalka, tel: (0554) 4 56 02...* ...g-standing Nessebur favourite serving seafood in a marvellous setting, with a terrace overlooking the sea.

VARNA

Hashove €€€ *1 bul Slivnitsa, tel: (052) 63 04 01.* Restaurant in the Odessos Hotel, which, while not serving the best food in Varna, certainly comes up with passable local dishes and seafood, and the location is the best in the city.

Kashtata €€ *7 bul Osmi Primorski Polk, tel: (052) 60 28 79.* Good choice of Bulgarian cuisine, including a fine selection of charcoal-grilled meats, barbecued outside in the huge garden.

Maestro €€ *4 ul Shipka, tel: (052) 61 45 14.* Bistro-type food and Varna's best pizzas are served in a large, open and spacious restaurant, whose upper level is about the best dining location in the city. Large terrace during the summer.

Morska Sirena €€ *47 bul Primorski, tel: (052) 69 20 96, <www. ran-bg.com>*. The most famous seafood restaurant on the entire coast, the Sirena is well known for its flair with fish and excellent standard of service.

Sherehadze €€ *4 ul Petko Karavelov, tel: (052) 64 22 93.* Fine Middle Eastern food in the heart the city. There are a large number of Turkish and Middle Eastern-type places in Varna and, while most should be avoided, this place is the genuine article.

INDEX

Berlitz pocket guide

Bulgaria

Second Edition 2008

Written by Craig Turp
Principal photographer: Pete Bennett
Edited by Alex Knights
Series Editor: Tony Halliday

Printed in Singapore by Insight Print
Services (Pte) Ltd, 38 Joo Koon Road,
Singapore 628990. Tel: (65) 6865-1600.
Fax: (65) 6861-6438

Berlitz Trademark Reg. U.S. Patent Office
and other countries. Marca Registrada

Photography credits
All photography by Pete Bennett, except page
36 (Reuters/Corbis) and page 80
(Skishoot–Offshoot).

Cover photograph: Kasia Nowak/Alamy

Contact us

At Berlitz we strive to keep our guides as
accurate and up to date as possible, but if you
find anything that has changed, or if you have
any suggestions on ways to improve this guide,
then we would be delighted to hear from you.

Berlitz Publishing, PO Box 7910,
London SE1 1WE, England.
fax: (44) 20 7403 0290
email: berlitz@apaguide.co.uk
www.berlitzpublishing.com